First World War
and Army of Occupation
War Diary
France, Belgium and Germany

7 INDIAN (MEERUT) DIVISION
Headquarters, Branches and Services
Commander Royal Artillery
1 January 1915 - 31 January 1915

WO95/3933/2

The Naval & Military Press Ltd
www.nmarchive.com
Published in association with The National Archives

Published by

The Naval & Military Press Ltd

Unit 10 Ridgewood Industrial Park,

Uckfield, East Sussex,

TN22 5QE England

Tel: +44 (0) 1825 749494

www.naval-military-press.com

www.nmarchive.com

This diary has been reprinted in facsimile from the original. Any imperfections are inevitably reproduced and the quality may fall short of modern type and cartographic standards.

© Crown Copyright
Images reproduced by permission of The National Archives, London, England, 2015.

Contents

Document type	Place/Title	Date From	Date To
Heading	Meerut Division H.Q. Div Art 1st to 28th Feb 1915		
Heading	War Diary With Appendices Head Quarters Divisional Artillery Meerut Division 1st February 1915 28th February 1915		
War Diary	Ham	01/02/1915	02/02/1915
War Diary	Locon	03/02/1915	13/02/1915
War Diary	Lillers	14/02/1915	25/02/1915
War Diary	Locon	26/02/1915	28/02/1915
Miscellaneous	Extract from 1st Corps Operations Order No.65 dated 30/1/15	30/01/1915	30/01/1915
Operation(al) Order(s)	Operation Order No.9 By Lieut Colonel L.A.C. Gordon Royal Field Artillery Commanding Royal Artillery Meerut Division	01/02/1915	01/02/1915
Miscellaneous	March Table Meerut Divisional Artillery	02/02/1915	02/02/1915
Miscellaneous	A Form Messages And Signals		
Operation(al) Order(s)	Operation Order No.15 By Lieutenant-General C.A. Anderson C,B. Commanding Meerut Division	01/02/1915	01/02/1915
Miscellaneous	A Form Messages And Signals		
Miscellaneous	Amendment To Meerut Divn Operation Order No.17 of 6/2/15	07/02/1915	07/02/1915
Operation(al) Order(s)	Operation Order No.17 By Lieutenant General C.A. Anderson C.B. Commanding Meerut Division	06/02/1915	06/02/1915
Miscellaneous	March Table		
Miscellaneous	A Form Messages And Signals		
Miscellaneous	O.L. 37th How: Battery R.F.A. 114th Heavy Battery R.G.A	09/02/1915	09/02/1915
Miscellaneous	A Form Messages And Signals		
Miscellaneous	216 R A (L)	09/02/1915	09/02/1915
Miscellaneous	A Form Messages And Signals		
Operation(al) Order(s)	Operation Order No.9 By Brigadier General A.B. Scott C.B. D.S.O. Commanding Royal Artillery Meerut Division	10/02/1915	10/02/1915
Miscellaneous	March Table Meerut Divisional Artillery		
Miscellaneous	B.M.582		
Miscellaneous	A Form Messages And Signals	15/02/1915	15/02/1915
Miscellaneous	List Of Hostile Batteries Opposite Meerut Divisional Artillery With Their Target Numbers And Map Positions		
Diagram etc	Diagram		
Miscellaneous	Messages Signals And Field Telegraphs	16/02/1915	16/02/1915
Miscellaneous	Appendix 103	18/02/1915	18/02/1915
Miscellaneous	A Form Messages And Signals		
Miscellaneous	Messages Signals And Field Telegraphs	18/02/1915	18/02/1915
Operation(al) Order(s)	Operation Order No.18 By Brigadier General A.B. Scott C.B. D.S.O. Commanding Meerut Division	20/02/1915	20/02/1915
Miscellaneous	March Table Annexure to Meerut Divn Operation Order No.18		
Miscellaneous	A Form Messages And Signals	23/02/1915	23/02/1915
Operation(al) Order(s)	Operation Order No.10 By Brigadier General H. St. C Lecky R.A. G.O.C. R.A. Meerut Division	24/02/1915	24/02/1915

Miscellaneous	March Table Meerut Divisional Artillery		
Miscellaneous	A Form Messages And Signals	28/02/1915	28/02/1915
Miscellaneous	Intelligence Summary Up to 11.p.m.	05/02/1915	05/02/1915
Miscellaneous	Intelligence Summary Up to 11.p.m.	06/02/1915	06/02/1915
Miscellaneous	Intelligence Summary Up to 10.30.p.m.	07/02/1915	07/02/1915
Miscellaneous	Intelligence Summary Up to 10.p.m.	08/02/1915	08/02/1915
Miscellaneous	Intelligence Summary Up to 11.p.m.	09/02/1915	09/02/1915
Miscellaneous	Intelligence Summary Up to 11.p.m.	10/02/1915	10/02/1915
Miscellaneous	Intelligence Summary Up to 11.p.m.	11/02/1915	11/02/1915
Miscellaneous	Intelligence Summary Up to 11.p.m.	12/02/1915	12/02/1915
Miscellaneous	Intelligence Summary Up to 11.p.m.	13/02/1915	13/02/1915
Miscellaneous	Intelligence Summary Up to 10.p.m.	26/02/1915	26/02/1915
Miscellaneous	Intelligence Summary Up to 11.p.m.	27/02/1915	27/02/1915
Miscellaneous	Intelligence Summary Up to 11.p.m.	28/02/1915	28/02/1915
Map	France (Bethune)		
Heading	Meerut Division 1st to 31st January 1915 C.R.A.		
Heading	War Diary of C.R.A. Meerut Division From 1st January 1915 To 31st January 1915		
War Diary	Ham	01/01/1915	31/01/1915
Miscellaneous	No.G 220/1 Headquarters Meerut Divn	22/01/1915	22/01/1915
Miscellaneous	No.G 220/2 Headquarters Meerut Divn	23/01/1914	23/01/1914
Miscellaneous	Headquarters Divisional Artillery Meerut Division	24/01/1915	24/01/1915
Map	France (Bethune)		
Heading	C.R.A. Meerut Divn Appendix 100		
Miscellaneous			
Miscellaneous	A Form Messages And Signals		
Miscellaneous	A Form Messages And Signals	25/01/1915	25/01/1915
Miscellaneous	Appendix 79		
Miscellaneous	To O.C. 110th (H) Btty R.E.A	25/01/1915	25/01/1915
Miscellaneous	A Form Messages And Signals	25/01/1915	25/01/1915

Meerut Division,

H.Q. DIV. ART.

1st To 28th Feb. 1915

Serial No. 65

12/4/15

M/7/3

with appendices.

Head Quarters, Divisional Artillery, Meerut Division.

From 1st February 1915 to 28th February 1915

Army Form C. 2118.

WAR DIARY VOLUME VII
or
INTELLIGENCE SUMMARY.
(Erase heading not required.)

Instructions regarding War Diaries and Intelligence Summaries are contained in F. S. Regs., Part II. and the Staff Manual respectively. Title pages will be prepared in manuscript.

Hour, Date, Place	Summary of Events and Information	Remarks and references to Appendices
6pm 1st February 1915. HAM.	So been issued with MEERUT Divion. N° 253/21-G dated 31.1.1915. Operation Order N° 8 by C.R.A. MEERUT Division were issued.	× Appendix 86.
	Information received from MEERUT Division that 37th How. Battery would be placed at disposal of MEERUT Division.	× Appendix 87
3.30 pm do.		∫ Appendix 88
	*Information received from MEERUT Division. Head INDIAN Corps	* appendix 89
5 pm do.	Instructions forward copies of Divisional Artillery MEERUT Division Operation Orders N° 13 received	⊗ appendix × 90.
2nd February 1915 HAM	MEERUT Division ound Artillery active.	NR 9.
8.30am 3rd February 1915 LOCON	Divisional Artillery Head quarters moved by march route to LOCON.	NR 9.
10 A.M. do.	Brigadier General A.B. SCOTT, C.B., D.S.O, who had been Commanding the MEERUT Detachment again assumed command of the MEERUT Divisional Artillery, and took over command of the 2nd Brigade R.A. Artillery at present in position on the line.	NR 9.
12 noon do.	11th Bde R.F.A. Ammn Column relieved 36th Bde R.F.A. Ammn Col.	
2 P.M. do.	11th Bde R.F.A. (two gun battery) relieved 36th Bde R.F.A, 66th Battery proceeding to billets at LA CIK MARNEUSE as reserve battery.	

Army Form C. 2118.

WAR DIARY
or
INTELLIGENCE SUMMARY.
(Erase heading not required.)

Instructions regarding War Diaries and Intelligence Summaries are contained in F.S. Regs., Part II. and the Staff Manual respectively. Title pages will be prepared in manuscript.

Hour, Date, Place	Summary of Events and Information	Remarks and references to Appendices
3rd February 1915. LOCON	Following hostile batteries reported active during the day:— 1. S.18.a 3.3 which fired on our trenches near crossroads in S.4.d. 2. Howitzer battery about A.5.a. 3. Howitzer battery in neighbourhood of VIOLAINES firing on FESTUBERT. 4. Field battery near VIOLAINES firing on RUE de L'EPINETTE. 5. Heavy battery S.E. of LORGIES (not located) firing towards FESTUBERT. 6. Battery at S.17c 9.9 or S.17c 4.4 which fired on our trenches in S.4.d.	
12 noon	9th. Battery and 2nd Siege Battery had a combined shoot on trenches in S.15.c	
12.53 p.m.	114th. Heavy Battery silenced hostile battery at VIOLAINES — 4 shell rapid. battery	
1. p.m.	70th. Batteries killed shelled by 5.9" howitzer, apparently intended for RUE des CHEVATTES	
1.20 p.m.	2nd Siege Battery located active field battery at T.25a and silenced it.	
1.40 p.m.	2nd Siege Battery shelled battery of 4 15.cm. Howitzers the firing on RUE des CHEVATTES from B.18. Replies process at 3.15.p.m. when this battery again opened fire and silenced it	
1.50 p.m.	35th. Heavy Battery engaged and silenced battery firing from S.18.a	
1.55 p.m.	114th. Heavy Battery fired on houses to RUE du MARAIS which appeared occupied — 7 direct hits on different houses	
2. p.m.	8th Siege Battery (6" guns) fired at gun located A.5 7 9.9 (VIOLAINES)	
3. p.m.	9th Battery obtained direct hit on machine gun emplaced S.15.t. 5.0.	
3.30 p.m.	35th Heavy Battery fired 11 rounds at heavy hostile battery in B.1.d — observation very difficult	

Army Form C. 2118.

WAR DIARY VOLUME VII
INTELLIGENCE SUMMARY.
(Erase heading not required.)

Instructions regarding War Diaries and Intelligence Summaries are contained in F. S. Regs, Part II. and the Staff Manual respectively. Title pages will be prepared in manuscript.

Hour, Date, Place	Summary of Events and Information	Remarks and references to Appendices
3.40 p.m. 3rd February 1915. LOCON.	114th Heavy Battery fired on hostile observing station near VIOLAINES with visual observation.	W.W.S.
6.a.m 4th February 1915. LOCON	During the afternoon the 4th Brigade R.J.A. relieved the 36th Bde R.J.A.	
	All quiet.	
9.15 a.m. do	114th Heavy Battery engaged battery at S 23 d 3.8, with aeroplane Range found.	
11.30 a.m. do	Battery at B1d was active, was engaged and silenced by 110th Heavy Battery visual observation.	
11.40 a.m. do	146th Battery R.J.A. saw men moving among houses near fork in S.11.a, shelled these houses obtaining four hits out of 6 rounds	
11.42 a.m. do	2nd Siege Battery engaged Howitzer Battery at B1d.	
11.55 a.m. do	35th Heavy Battery fired a few rounds at Distillery, now located A 62 1.9 110th Heavy Battery fired on enemys battery at S 28 C 9.10, and obtained range.	
12.4 p.m. do	114th Heavy Battery fired on battery at BEAU-PUITS – S 30 d 2.8 with aeroplane observation.	
2.5 p.m. do	2nd Siege register on machine gun emplacement at S.16 d 3.10	
2.40 p.m. do	114th Heavy Battery engaged LA BASSEE observation post, obtained a direct hit with 4th round.	
2.47 p.m. do	2nd Siege shelled Redoubt at S.15.C.	
3.30 p.m. do	35th Heavy Battery fired 8 rounds at active hostile battery at S.30 & 8.8. and located it firing. 110th Heavy Battery engaged battery at S.29.d.5.0. with aeroplane observation but only found bracket.	

Army Form C. 2118.

WAR DIARY
or
INTELLIGENCE SUMMARY.
(Erase heading not required.)

Instructions regarding War Diaries and Intelligence Summaries are contained in F.S. Regs., Part II. and the Staff Manual respectively. Title pages will be prepared in manuscript.

Hour, Date, Place	Summary of Events and Information	Remarks and references to Appendices
4 p.m. 4th February 1915. LOCON.	A 15 cm H.E. shell burst in yard of 13th Brigade Head Quarter billet, killed the Brigade Trumpeter and wounded 3 men of Brigade Staff; 4 horses also wounded.	
5.20 p.m. do	14th Battery R.F.A. silenced enemys machine gun.	
5.25 p.m. do	14th Battery fired on enemys trenches in S10d at request of Infantry who were carrying out reliefs.	
	At about 2 p.m. the 9th Brigade R.F.A. (less 19th Battery) arrived at LE TOURET and relieved 41st Bde of 2nd Divisional Artillery, and the 13th Brigade R.F.A. (less 8th Battery in reserve) relieved 34th Bde R.F.A. near LA COUTURE.	
	The 12th Section Anti-Aircraft (18 pr.) arrived during the morning and went into action near LA COUTURE.	+ Appendix 9/
	MEERUT Divisional Ammunition Column, which marched to PARADIS from NEDONCHELLE yesterday, took up the supply of ammunition from 12 noon today.	WDg
	Orders were received for 35th Heavy Battery to relieve 113th Heavy Battery during the 5th and 6th.	
	During the day the Brigade Major R.A. of the 8th Division came to discuss possibilities of combined Artillery work between the two divisions.	
5th February 1915. LOCON	A fair bright morning, which gave indications of being a good day for Aerial observation.	
6 a.m. do	All reported quiet.	
8.35 a.m. do	35th Heavy Battery fired 4 rounds at Shrine Redoubt (S.26.3-3.2)	
9 a.m. do	A German aeroplane dropped a striped orange and white paper balloon over the 8th Siege Battery.	
9.30 a.m. do	35th Heavy Battery fired 5 rounds at hostile battery in T.25a, which was active at intervals during the day.	

Army Form C. 2118.

WAR DIARY Volume VII
INTELLIGENCE SUMMARY.
(Erase heading not required.)

Instructions regarding War Diaries and Intelligence Summaries are contained in F. S. Regs., Part II. and the Staff Manual respectively. Title pages will be prepared in manuscript.

Hour, Date, Place	Summary of Events and Information	Remarks and references to Appendices
10 a.m. 5th February 1915 LOCON	114th Battery fired at an enemy post in SW corner of S.20.T. Shoe it in view with salvo/motor rounds.	
10.9 a.t. do	35th Heavy Battery fired 10 rounds at battery at S.30.b reported active by observed officer in RUE du BOIS. 114th Heavy Battery engaged new gun emplacement at B7a 10.8 with aeroplane observation. Range and hit reported correct at 6th round. Two bursts of fire noted at it.	
11.5 a.m. do	Orders received from MEERUT Division for 18 pr Anti Aircraft gun to march as soon as possible to BAILLEUL.	+ Appendix 92
11.47 a.m. do	114th Heavy Battery registered on VIOLAINES and engaged battery at A.5.b.	
12.30 p.m. do	G.O.C. R.A LAHORE Division with his Brigade Major came during the morning & three Artillery are sent to	
1.15 p.m. do	35th Heavy Battery put 12 rounds into enemy trenches at S.21.a.8.6.	
2 p.m. do	N: 12 Section Anti Aircraft (one 18 pr) marched out en route for BAILLEUL	
2 p.m. do	114th Heavy Battery calibrated guns on VIOLAINES.	
3 p.m. do	G.O.C. R.A attended conference at BETHUNE in connection with cooperation with 2nd Division's attack on 6th February	
6.30 p.m. do	114th Heavy Battery engaged hostile battery at BEAUPUITS (S.302) and observed range. Right Section 35th Heavy Battery marched out and was relieved by a Section of the 113th Heavy Battery. Conference of O.C's Heavy Batteries at which G.O.C. R.A. allotted tasks for cooperation with 2nd Division's attack on 6.2.15.	

Army Form C. 2118.

WAR DIARY (Vol XII)
or
INTELLIGENCE SUMMARY.
(Erase heading not required.)

Instructions regarding War Diaries and Intelligence Summaries are contained in F. S. Regs., Part II. and the Staff Manual respectively. Title pages will be prepared in manuscript.

Hour, Date, Place	Summary of Events and Information	Remarks and references to Appendices
5th February 1915 LOCON	During the day the vicinity of RICHEBOURG ST VAAST was shelled frequently from vicinity of BOIS du BIEZ. Artillery in vicinity of BEAU PUITS and VIOLAINES was also active. Hostile guns were noticed in enemy trenches during the day. Daily Intelligence Summary to attached as an Appendix.	NW9.
6 a.m. 6th February 1915. LOCON	All quiet.	
7.30 a.m. do	14th Battery shelled party of 30 germans crossing barricade in S5c.	
11.15 a.m. do	2nd Battery shelled White Patch House (S.11.c.4.4)	
11.30 a.m. do	44th Battery shelled enemy works in S.20.t. (taking them in partial enfilade) in conjunction with 2nd Siege Battery	
11.50 a.m. do	2nd Siege Battery registered on S.16.a.5.0.	
12 noon do	Battery at 6a × ~~S.5 a~~ active and engaged by 110th Heavy Battery and again at 1.25 p.m.	× Appendix – Map.
	14th Battery shelled some germans out of a house in S.11.7 which they had been seen to enter.	
12.18 a.m. do	35th Heavy Battery (remaining section) engaged active hostile battery at RUE du MARAIS and silenced it.	
1.30 pm & 2.15 pm } do	9th and 13th Brigades R.F.A. carried fire with bursts of fire during bombardment of enemy position near GIVENCHY.	
2. P.M. do	7th Battery observing station shelled by enemy and had to be vacated. Major PARRINGTON slightly wounded in the head	

Army Form C. 2118.

WAR DIARY
or
INTELLIGENCE SUMMARY.
(Erase heading not required.)

Instructions regarding War Diaries and Intelligence Summaries are contained in F.S. Regs., Part II. and the Staff Manual respectively. Title pages will be prepared in manuscript.

Hour, Date, Place	Summary of Events and Information	Remarks and references to Appendices
2 p.m. to 2.15 p.m. 6th February 1915. LOCON	110th Heavy Battery, 114th Heavy Battery, 2nd & 8th Siege Batteries bombarded areas allotted to them at conference last night, viz: 110th Heavy Battery { Battery at B.7.a. 4.5 (5b) / Battery at B.7.a. 5.5 (11) } ⟶ { 2 guns on Railway triangle with orders for one gun to hang there. One South to AUCHY. } 114th Heavy Battery { 1 gun on A.12.d. 8.4 (4) / 1 gun on S.30.d. 2.9 (5) } 2nd Siege Battery { Crossroads at CANTALEUX / Battery at VIOLAINES A.5 & 9.5 (4c) } 8th Siege Battery { 2 guns on East half of "Railway Triangle" / 1 gun on VIOLAINES } Fire was kept up at a brisk rate during this quarter of an hour. One 6" gun of 8th Siege Battery obtained the high rate of 21 rds in 15 mins.	⟶ Appendix 10. Rep.
2.15 p.m.	37th Howitzer Battery opened fire on enemy Redoubt near "Riquet Maison" on account of rifle fire which had silenced 110th Heavy Battery's observation post in RUE du BOIS. was shelled from direction of S.30.d.2.9.(5)	
2.15 p.m. to 3 p.m.	Weight appeared approx. 60 lbs N.17 received. The Heavy Batteries shewn above fired occasional bursts of fire at the above areas.	Capt +92a
3.50 p.m.	Attack on Brickfields W. of triangle has been successful, but think enemy Artillery is active. Orders telephoned out to Heavy Batteries to be prepared to neutralize any battery observed to be active.	
4.2 p.m.	Information received that enemy were in force in Railway cutting & also noise to 114th Heavy Battery and 8th Siege Battery to shell it.	

Army Form C. 2118.

WAR DIARY
or
INTELLIGENCE SUMMARY.
(Erase heading not required.)

Instructions regarding War Diaries and Intelligence Summaries are contained in F.S. Regs., Part II. and the Staff Manual respectively. Title pages will be prepared in manuscript.

Hour, Date, Place	Summary of Events and Information	Remarks and references to Appendices
4.6. p.m. 6th February 1915. LOCON.	114th Heavy Battery and 8th Siege Battery fired on triangle and later 114th H.B. lengthened out to A/V/C.H.Y. where 2 battalions were reported. 8th Siege and 114th H.B. were also ordered to fire on cross roads on A.18.b. 6.8. and battery at A.12.d. 8.4(u) while 110th H.B. fired on A.12.d. 8.4(u) & are also at hostile batteries reported active at S.17.d. 6.(5) & S.18.a. 5.3. (4b) Second section of 113th Heavy Battery arrived at position vacated by 35th Heavy Battery after dark. During the day direct through telephonic communication was arranged by the Indian Corps from the 2nd Divisional Artillery office to the Meerut Divisional Artillery office – a line was also established from the Meerut Divisional Artillery office to the Meerut Signal office, whence the line could be plugged into the 8th Division and thence to 8th Divisional Artillery. Telephonic communication with G.O.C., R.A. on either flank of the Meerut Division was thus obtained. Daily Intelligence Summary is attached as an Appendix	

Army Form C. 2118.

WAR DIARY
or
INTELLIGENCE SUMMARY.
(Erase heading not required.)

Hour, Date, Place	Summary of Events and Information	Remarks and references to Appendices
7th February 1915. LOCON		
6. a.m.	All quiet. Thick and cloudy morning unfavourable for aeroplane work.	
7.10 a.m. to 8.45 a.m.	2nd Siege Battery fired 11 rounds H.L. at LONE TREE TRENCH (S.21.a.9.6)	
8. a.m.	14th Battery shelled enemy barricade in S.5a which a party of enemy were seen crossing	
10. a.m.	Hostile battery shelled trenches in S.10.a.7. but desisted as soon as 7th Battery shelled Distillery (51) S.17.a.7.4.	
10.30 a.m.	20th Battery shelled enemy infantry driven out of trenches by fire of 2nd Siege Battery.	
10.35 a.m. to 11. a.m. 11.10. a.m.	2nd Siege again fired at S.21.a.9.6, 30 H foot shell but no 4th Battery fired on germans seen working in trench in S.20.7 2nd Siege fired 11 rounds at enemy battery in B.1.d.	
2. p.m. to 2.30.p.m.	8th Siege (6" gun) registered on white house (S.16.a.5.0) obtaining a direct hit.	
2.30 p.m.	2nd Siege Battery fired on machine gun emplaced at S.16.a.9.1. 20th Battery fired on heads seen moving in trench at S.15.c, and afterwards turned on to trench in S.15.7 as rifle fire was worrying our trench picquets.	
3. p.m.	2nd Battery fired on enemy communication trenches at S.17.c. 114th Heavy Battery registered on VIOLAINES O.P and obtained 2 direct hits	
4. p.m.	7th Battery observation station shelled - presumably by S.17.d.6.6.(52) but possibly by S.30.d.2.9.(5) the 7th Battery R.F.A. and 110th Heavy Battery engaged former in conjunction, and shelling stopped	

Army Form C. 2118.

WAR DIARY
or
INTELLIGENCE SUMMARY.
(Erase heading not required.)

Instructions regarding War Diaries and Intelligence Summaries are contained in F.S. Regs, Part II. and the Staff Manual respectively. Title pages will be prepared in manuscript.

Hour, Date, Place	Summary of Events and Information	Remarks and references to Appendices
4.5. p.m. 7th February 1915 LOCON	As very heavy firing heard from direction of GIVENCHY. 8th Siege Battery was ordered to turn fire of one gun on Eastern edge of Railway triangle.	
4.7. p.m. do	114th Heavy Battery was ordered to turn one gun on to triangle, one gun on to A.12.d.8.4 and one gun on to VIOLAINES (sh)	
4.10. p.m. do	110th Heavy Battery was ordered to turn one gun on to B.7a.4.5 and one gun on B1.d.5.5 (17)	
4.11. p.m. do	2nd Siege Battery ordered to turn one gun on to CANTALEUX.	
4.35. p.m. do	Hostile firing slackened down, fire of active batteries ordered to cease	
4.40 pm to 4.50.p.m. do	At 114th Heavy Battery ordered to continue slow fire on VIOLAINES and A.12.d.8.4 and then stop.	
	Daily Intelligence Summary is attached as an Appendix.	

Army Form C. 2118.

WAR DIARY
or
INTELLIGENCE SUMMARY.
(Erase heading not required.)

Instructions regarding War Diaries and Intelligence Summaries are contained in F. S. Regs., Part II. and the Staff Manual respectively. Title pages will be prepared in manuscript.

Hour, Date, Place	Summary of Events and Information	Remarks and references to Appendices
8th February 1915. LOCON	A fine clear morning but a very strong wind blowing.	
8.30 a.m.	114th Battery fired on salvoes of rock in S20a and Redoubt S20d O.5.	
9.30 a.m.	114th Heavy Battery engaged enemy battery at BEAU PUITS (S30d 2.9) with aerial observation and obtained range correctly.	
10 a.m.	7th Battery's observation post was shelled.	
10.10 a.m.	2nd Siege Battery registered on LONE TREE TRENCH - S21 a 9.6.	
	G.O.C., R.A rode round the Northern batteries and interviewed R.A. Group Commdr. Northern Section, reference operation against a barricade.	
10.30 a.m.	114th Heavy Battery fired on LA BASSEE Observing Station. 10 rds. 1 hit recorded.	
12 noon	Railway Engine seen puffing smoke in N. direction behind ILLIES as seen from S9 a 6.4.	
12.28 p.m.	114th Heavy Battery with aerial observation fired at suspicious house at S22 7.5.3. obtaining 3 hits out of 11 shots.	
12.30 p.m.	2nd Siege fired 25 rounds at VIOLAINES Church, 1 hit recorded but several other buildings hit.	
1 p.m.	37th How Battery fired on working party in Redoubt near PIQUET House and made a rift of 4' or 6' in the parapet.	
2.25 p.m.	114th Heavy Battery registered on VIOLAINES.	
2.30 p.m.	7th Battery's observation post again shelled.	
2.55 p.m.	114th Heavy fired 8 rounds at VIOLAINES Observation Station.	
3.10 p.m.	2nd Battery fired at horses in S11 c 4.4. where considerable movement was seen.	
3.35 p.m.	114th Heavy Battery engaged battery 6a (S28 7.9.10) while observing for PONTE FIXE also a few rounds at distillery in VIOLAINES - A6 a 10.6	
4 P.M.	8th Large Battery fired a few rounds at VIOLAINES Battery at A6 7 5.1	
4.30 p.m.	A short sharp contrast bombardment of VIOLAINES Battery and 8th Siege Battery took place - 110th & 114th Heavy Batteries and 8th Siege Battery Co-operating.	

Army Form C. 2118.

WAR DIARY
or
INTELLIGENCE SUMMARY.
(Erase heading not required.)

Instructions regarding War Diaries and Intelligence Summaries are contained in F.S. Regs., Part II. and the Staff Manual respectively. Title pages will be prepared in manuscript.

Hour, Date, Place	Summary of Events and Information	Remarks and references to Appendices
8th February 1915 LOCON	During the day 6a (S.28.b.9.10) and 52 (S.17.d.6.6) were both fired at by Moat Heavy Battery — their activity being suspected. Same battery also fired occasional rounds at the Distillery (S.17.a.7.4) during the day. 113th Heavy Battery proceeded with registration during the day — 57th How. Battery registered various trenches — During the day information received from MEERUT Division that 11th Heavy Battery was to be transferred to 5th Corps	*Appendix G3 MWE
Midnight 8th/9th February 1915 LOCON	37th How. Battery + 114th Heavy Battery Daily Intelligence Summary to attached. on enemy working party in S.21 and S.20 under an 44th Battery fired on enemy working party in S.21 and S.20 under an arrangement made with O.C. Suffolk Regt.	
9th February 1915 LOCON	Wet and stormy morning, with no chance of any aerial observation during day.	
7.50.a.m. do.	114th Battery fired on a M.G. in S.10.z and hit parapet.	
8.30.a.m. do.	Same battery fired 4 rounds at working parties carrying large planks across barricade S.5.c. M.G. officer reported 4 men fell out of 6.	
9.a.m. do.	Enemy shelled RUE du BOIS and 7th Battery O.P.	
9.30.a.m. do.	110th Heavy Battery fired at 4 likely observing stations to try and stop this fire.	
9.50 a.m. do.	114th Heavy Battery fired at the LA BASSEE and VIOLAINES Stations — also at battery at A.6.b.5.1.	
10.15. a.m. do.	4 shell reported as 77 m.m. field gun shrapnel fell near observation station of 44th Battery in R.UE du BOIS — bearing about 137° (S.28.b.9.10?)	
10.45 a.m. do.	20th Battery fired 9 rounds "searching" for light howitzer which had been firing on RUE du BOIS.	
11 a.m. do.	Trenches N. of Bunnery shelled by enemy. Weather too thick to locate batteries firing.	

WAR DIARY or INTELLIGENCE SUMMARY.

Army Form C. 2118.

(Erase heading not required.)

Instructions regarding War Diaries and Intelligence Summaries are contained in F.S. Regs, Part II. and the Staff Manual respectively. Title pages will be prepared in manuscript.

Hour, Date, Place	Summary of Events and Information	Remarks and references to Appendices
11.15 am 9th February 1915 LOCON	44th Battery shelled Salient in S.29.f — one H.E. shell burst among a cluster of Germans — causing dispersal, but effect not known.	
11.15 to 11.45 a.m.	56th How. Battery fired 13 rounds at intervals at School house (S.22.a.1.9.) and house at S.17c 10.0.	
11.25 am	114th Heavy Battery fired at battery at S.28 & 9.10x and also a few rounds (6a) at battery in Orchard at S.30 d 2.9 (5)	
12.30 p.m.	28th Battery fired a few rounds at German Redoubt in front of PIQUET House.	
12.55 p.m.	114th Battery registered BOIS du BIEZ	
1.00 p.m.	114th Battery fired at house S.11.a.9.4. and obtained a direct hit.	
1.25 p.m.	114th Battery fired 7 rounds at house S.11.7.1.1. Suspected of being an Observation Station to gun reported by infantry to be in orchard behind it. Two H.E. struck house and appeared to have very good effect on the structure. Third fell on out buildings behind.	
2.50 p.m.	114th Battery fired on M.G. emplacement in enemys trench with H.E. — effect appeared good.	
4.8 p.m.	114th Heavy Battery fired at VIOLAINES observation station and obtained 2 hits, and also on hostile active battery at A.6 & 5.1.	
4.15 p.m.	20th Battery fired 8 rounds on apparently new machine gun emplacement S.15 a 8.0.	
4.30 p.m.	28th Battery fired a few rounds at a tall red house in RUE d'OUVERT, Suspected of being a billet – 2 shell burst inside this house. 114th Battery saw a party carrying sandbags across barricade S.5a and at 4 ST. fired 2 rounds at this barricade.	
4.45 to 5.15 p.m.	Enemy's artillery searched ground between 9th Bgde HdQrs and Cse de RAUX, using black powder shell Moreover during the day 110 lb Heavy Battery dropped occasional rounds into DISTILLERY (S.17a 74) and WHITE House (S.16 & 5.0) suspected of being Observing stations. The 8th Regt. also registered on WHITE House. Further information contained in Daily Summary Intelligence Summary to attached as an Appendix.	

Army Form C. 2118.

WAR DIARY
or
INTELLIGENCE SUMMARY.
(Erase heading not required.)

Instructions regarding War Diaries and Intelligence Summaries are contained in F.S. Regs., Part II. and the Staff Manual respectively. Title pages will be prepared in manuscript.

Hour, Date, Place	Summary of Events and Information	Remarks and references to Appendices
6.a.m. 10th February 1915 LOCON	Very thick - all quiet.	
7. a.m. do	Fine clear morning but a little mist low down. Light wind gave promise of a good day for aerial observation.	
7.15 a.m. do	14th Battery fired at party of enemy crossing barricade in S6C. 110th Heavy Battery with aerial observation registered on farm at Le PLOUICH, in anticipation of a combined bombardment with 8th Division.	
10.35 to 11.20 am 11.30 am do } do	7th Battery carried on registration. 114th Heavy Battery with aeroplane observation engaged 6a (S.28 & 9.10). Range quickly found and something blown up — probably a limber. 2nd Siege Battery shelled barricade in S.10. & 8.6 with good effect, the parapit being completely breached —	✗ Appendix 100 — Map
11.45 a.m. do	7th Battery co-operated in above operation with 2nd Siege Battery.	
12.30. p.m. do	14th Battery fired on same barricade at party of men carrying planks, and wheeling barrows, causing some casualties.	
1.45 p.m. do	A light field gun fired a few rounds at PORT ARTHUR.	✗ Appendix 94
1.45 p.m. do	Orders received for 37th Howitzer Battery and 113th Heavy Battery to be transferred to IVth Corps forthwith.	
1.53. p.m. do	2nd Siege Battery fired 5 rounds at the SHRINE Redoubt.	
2.40 p.m. do	Enemy battery (5) S.30.A.2.9. opened fire at the "RITZ", was engaged and silenced by 110th Heavy Battery.	
2.45 p.m. do	7th Battery reported observation Station shelled, battery doing it not located. 2nd Siege Battery fired 16 rounds heavy lyddite at Redoubt S.10.T.	
3.45. p.m. do	N: 5″ gun opened fire and was again silenced by 110th Howitzer Battery 28th Battery and 37th How Battery fired in conjunction on Redoubt just N.W. of Orchard.	
4.15. p.m. do	RUE du BOIS shelled by enemy's artillery.	
4.20 p.m. do	do.	
	do.	

Army Form C. 2118.

WAR DIARY
or
INTELLIGENCE SUMMARY.
(Erase heading not required.)

Instructions regarding War Diaries and Intelligence Summaries are contained in F. S. Regs., Part II. and the Staff Manual respectively. Title pages will be prepared in manuscript.

Hour, Date, Place	Summary of Events and Information	Remarks and references to Appendices
4 p.m. 10th February 1915. LOCON.	Heavy German Howitzer firing into S 10 C reported from direction of NEUVE CHAPELLE	
4.15 p.m. do	110th Heavy Battery and 114th Heavy Battery opened a counter bombardment of enemy's battery (N° 37) at S.30.d.2.9.	
5.15 p.m. do	Enemy's light howitzer fired a few rounds on RUE du BOIS S.9.	
7 p.m. do	Operation Order N° 9 issued for the relief of MEERUT Divisional Artillery.	*Appendix 95*
	During the day 8th Siege Battery registered on Distillery (S.17.a.8.3) and obtained 4 direct hits. 56th How. Battery registered on hostile trenches S.15.2.8. and S.10.7.3.8.	* M2.S
6 a.m. 11th February 1915 LOCON.	For fuller daily intelligence summary see attached as an Appendix. Very thick. All quiet. A little aerial work was carried out during the morning, but it was only clear enough for this at intervals. Unfortunately the "wireless" aeroplane working with 8th Siege Battery had engine troubles and missed the best part of the day.	
10.30 a.m. do	2nd Siege Battery in conjunction with 114th Battery R.F.A. shelled Redoubt in S.10.7. near Pumping Station - one good direct made.	
11 a.m. do	114th Battery fired at Salient in S.20. a. H.E. shell exploded in the end of a Splinter proof and caused Germans to retire from there -	x Appendix 100 leap.
11.30 a.m. do	2nd Battery's old position in RUE des CHEVATTES was shelled with 5" rounds from enemy's 15 c.m. howitzer.	
12.15 a.m. do	The "RITZ" factory was shelled by enemy 5.9" gun from E. side of BOIS du BIEZ 2nd Siege Battery and 2nd Battery R.F.A. shelled Redoubt in S.10.a.8.8. – reported very effective. Enemy shelled "RITZ" – believed to be either by H.V. gun in direction of BEAU PUITS 5:6 at 5.2" shells ceased within DISTILLERY (57), 5- and 6a	
12.25 p.m. do	DISTILLERY (57) shelled by 56th How. 15" Battery in conjunction with 44th Battery R.F.A. were all simultaneously shelled by us in reply.	

Army Form C. 2118.

WAR DIARY
or
INTELLIGENCE SUMMARY.
(Erase heading not required.)

Instructions regarding War Diaries and Intelligence Summaries are contained in F.S. Regs, Part II. and the Staff Manual respectively. Title pages will be prepared in manuscript.

Hour, Date, Place	Summary of Events and Information	Remarks and references to Appendices
12.30 p.m. 11th February 1915. LOCON	114th Battery R.F.A. shelled splinter proof in front line trenches at S.15.d.3.7 using H.E. shell with good effect, also in conjunction with 56th How: Battery.	
2. p.m. do	20th Battery fired a few rounds at trench S.15.c.8.2	
2.30 p.m. do	Redoubt in S.10.d.6.8 again shelled – several Germans have returned in the interval to repair it – effect good.	
2.45 p.m. do	20th Battery R.F.A. shelled Machine Gun emplacement S.15.a.8.3.	
3. p.m. do	114th Battery observed flashes at S.S.d. – doubt less battery at S.5.d. 5.5. – this was engaged by 110th Heavy Battery during the morning with aerial observation.	
3.35 p.m. do	2nd Siege Battery ~~engaged~~ shelled Sabaret in S.20.b.10.4 – not round very effective.	
3.40 p.m. do	Enemy shelled observing station in RUE du BOIS – No.5. inspected – shelled by 110th Heavy Battery.	
	Enemy appeared very quiet in front of Southern section of our line all day. Infantry report having seen many wounded being along trench after yesterdays bombardment of barricade at S.10.b.8.6. Copy of daily Intelligence Summary is attached as an Appendix.	MM 9

Army Form C. 2118.

WAR DIARY
or
INTELLIGENCE SUMMARY.
(Erase heading not required.)

Instructions regarding War Diaries and Intelligence Summaries are contained in F.S. Regs., Part II. and the Staff Manual respectively. Title pages will be prepared in manuscript.

Hour, Date, Place	Summary of Events and Information	Remarks and references to Appendices
12th February 1915 LOCON	Very thick in early morning, observation quite impossible.	
7.45 a.m. do.	Very heavy gun fire heard in direction of CUINCHY	
7.55 a.m. do.	114th Battery fired at working party on barricade in S.5.d	
9.55 a.m. do.	Observation station of 7th Battery now shelled.	
10 a.m. do.	G.O.C. LAHORE Division assumed command of this line from G.O.C. MEERUT DIVISION.	
	114th Battery shelled Salient in S.20 with H.E. with effect on splinter proof.	
10.15 a.m. do.	Same battery fired a few shell into Redoubt in S.20.	
10.30 a.m. do.	2nd Siege Battery fired 5 rounds at Battery No 5, which persistently shelled the "RITZ" all through the day.	Appendix 180 Sep
12. noon do.	7th Battery in conjunction with 2nd Siege shelled Redoubt in S.10.d. Hostile field battery from direction of 52, shelled the RUE du BOIS. 20th Battery fired at new work in S.15.c.85.	
12.45 p.m. do.	7th Battery and 2nd Siege Battery again shelled Redoubt in S.10.d, so Germans had returned to it. Fire reported very effective.	
12.50 p.m. do.	110th Heavy Battery fired at H6 and E8 reported active.	
1 p.m. do.	114th Heavy Battery registered on VIOLAINES and shelled the O.P. there.	
1.45 p.m. do.	Combined bombardment took place of Redoubt in S.10.A. by 114th, 7th, 2nd 114th Field Batteries, 56th How. Battery and 2nd Siege Battery. Burns, this time by previous arrangement, the 110th and 114th Heavy Batteries kept up a slow fire on probable hostile observation posts at WHITE HOUSE the Distillery VIOLAINES DISTILLERY also O.P. battery at S.11.c. 4.2" battery at S.28.7. 9.10 Jutland battery at S.30.d.2.95)th kept the fire of these down during this operation (G) effect reported very poor.	
2 p.m. do.	Battery at S.30.d.2.9 opened fire on RITZ and was promptly engaged by 110th Heavy Battery.	
2.20 p.m. do.	Still very thick. No chance of work by airman.	
2.30 p.m. do.	O.P. of 2nd Battery shelled	
3 p.m. do.	O.P. of 2nd Battery shelled	

Army Form C. 2118.

WAR DIARY
or
INTELLIGENCE SUMMARY.
(Erase heading not required.)

Instructions regarding War Diaries and Intelligence Summaries are contained in F.S. Regs., Part II. and the Staff Manual respectively. Title pages will be prepared in manuscript.

Hour, Date, Place	Summary of Events and Information	Remarks and references to Appendices
12th February 1915. LOCON		
3.10 p.m.	110th Heavy Battery fired 3 rounds at Likely Observation house in S 24 & 8.2 and hit it heavily with 3rd Shot.	
3.50 p.m. do	2nd Siege Battery fired on Shrine Redoubt, with very good effect.	
4.20 p.m. do	O.P. of 2nd Battery shelled.	
5 p.m. do	G.O.C. R.A. MEERUT Division accompanied by the Brigade Major R.A. went to LA GORGUE to arrange details for a combined operations with 8th Divisional Artillery on 13.2.15.	
	Copy of the Daily Intelligence Summary is attached as an Appendix.	M.Q.S.
13th February 1915. LOCON	The day opened very stormy, with a high wind and rain squalls. Work with aeroplanes for the day improbable.	
9.30 a.m. do	44th Battery fired a few rounds at machine gun emplacement in S.14-d.26.	
10 a.m. to 10.15 am do	2nd Siege Battery with previous plan arranged upon work with G.O.C. R.A. 8th Division at LA GORGUE last night, the heavy batteries opened fire on neighbourhood of BAS POMMERAU and Le PLOUICH as follows:-
110th Heavy Battery on Le PLOUICH farm (previously registered with aeroplane) and two hostile battery positions in that neighbourhood.
114th Heavy Battery on hostile position at POMMEREAU - T.1.3.10.0 (by map)
8th Siege Battery (6" guns) on BAS POMMEREAU gun positions S.32 c 5.5 to S.32 e 7.5.5. (by map).
A rapid rate of fire was maintained for a quarter of an hour all the heavy batteries of 7th and 8th Divisions, also participating in this operation. The result of which is at present unknown as no aeroplane was able to watch it.	
10.30 A. 2. 29 6)	114th Heavy Battery engaged number 5.
44th Battery fired H.E. shell at Lubrick in S. 20, also at new building shelter 175° S. of Sabrick, a few German left the shelter after it was hit.	*Appendix 100. Map
Form/C. 2118/10

Army Form C. 2118.

WAR DIARY
or
INTELLIGENCE SUMMARY.
(Erase heading not required.)

Instructions regarding War Diaries and Intelligence Summaries are contained in F.S. Regs., Part II. and the Staff Manual respectively. Title pages will be prepared in manuscript.

Hour, Date, Place	Summary of Events and Information	Remarks and references to Appendices
12 noon 13th February 1915 LOCON	10th Brigade of LAHORE Division relieved the 14th Bde R.F.A. which withdrew to billets at LA BRASSERIE, with the exception that the 83rd Battery of LAHORE Division remained in billets at ST FLORIS owing to a case of suspected Cerebro Meningitis.	
12 noon to 1 p.m. do	The 19th Battery remained on in reserve at LA CUX MAMEUSE to support the 9th Brigade R.F.A. vice 83rd Battery. The 5th Brigade R.F.A. relieved the 9th Brigade at LE TOURET (except 19th Battery). Both 9th + 5th Brigade Batteries fired a few registering rounds during the afternoon.	
12.15 p.m. do	2nd Siege Battery fired 5 rounds heavy lyddite at Redoubt in S.18.c.	
1 p.m. do	2nd Siege Battery fired 5 rounds at Salhoir near Orchard S.20 & 10.4.	
1.20 p.m. do	N°.7 shelled the "RITZ" (O.P.) and 110th Heavy Battery engaged it, also 6", O.P. House at LORGIES and 5.2*	+ Appear dne 150. — MSp.
1.30 p.m. do	110th Heavy Battery fired 10 rounds at VIOLAINES observation station.	
2 a.m. do	2nd Siege Battery fired at battery b4, which ceased firing.	
2.5 p.m. do	110th Heavy Battery fired 9 rounds at S?	
2.25 p.m. do	The House E of "RITZ" was fired on, this the "RITZ" itself, one shell blowing down the roadway the house W of "RITZ". While these were taking place shots were observed from a battery in S.24 & 2.8. which was probably the offender. 110th Heavy Battery engaged this, firing 26 C.P. shell at it. ½ rounds appeared most effective, 2 of them sending up showers of sparks.	
2.51 p.m. do	2nd Siege Battery fired 9 rounds at LONE TREE TRENCH. S.21.9.6.	
3.45 p.m. do	110th Heavy Battery engaged N° 4C which has "searching" for this battery.	

Army Form C. 2118.

WAR DIARY
or
INTELLIGENCE SUMMARY.
(Erase heading not required.)

Instructions regarding War Diaries and Intelligence Summaries are contained in F.S. Regs., Part II. and the Staff Manual respectively. Title pages will be prepared in manuscript.

Hour, Date, Place	Summary of Events and Information	Remarks and references to Appendices
5. p.m. 13th February 1915. LOCON	For information re hostile batteries active during the day, see Intelligence summary dated 13.2.15* attached. During the day the G.O.C. R.A. 2nd Division and his Brigade Major visited the G.O.C. R.A. MEERUT Division to talk over cooperation of MEERUT Divisional Artillery with that of the 2nd Division and the trench in a minor operation or morning of 14th. Vide SECRET Memo. The Heavy Batteries received their representatives to received orders + instructions in connection with the above. Later 2nd Divisional B.M. 587 secret instructions with reference to above operation received. During the afternoon the weather cleared somewhat, and it was hoped that work with aeroplane observation with Heavy Batteries would be possible. 2 Machines succeeded in ascending, but observation work proved impossible.	*Appendix 95a JMQ 9.
14th February 1915. LILLERS.	The day opened rough and stormy and aeroplane work again rendered impossible.	
10.a.m. to 10.7 p.m.	The Heavy Batteries was previously arranged opened a rapid fire on objectives allotted to them at Conference last night. These were as follows:-	x Appendix 100. Sheets

110th Heavy Battery { 1 Section on battery 17j +
  „ „ 1 „ „ „ 36 +
114th „ „ { 1 gun on VIOLAINE S battery 43 +
  „ „ 1 „ „ LA BASSEE „ 41 +
  „ „ 1 „ „ BEAU PUITS 5.
2nd Siege „ { 1 Section on X Roads at CANTALEUX
  „ „ 1 gun on 6A +
  „ „ 1 gun on 4C +
8th Siege „ { 1 Section on Eastern half of Railway Triangle
  „ „ 1 gun on VIOLAINE S battery at 43 +

Forms/C. 2118/10

Army Form C. 2118.

WAR DIARY
or
INTELLIGENCE SUMMARY.
(Erase heading not required.)

Instructions regarding War Diaries and Intelligence Summaries are contained in F.S. Regs., Part II. and the Staff Manual respectively. Title pages will be prepared in manuscript.

Hour, Date, Place	Summary of Events and Information	Remarks and references to Appendices
10.15 to 10.30am 14th February 1915 LILLERS	Above batteries maintained a desultory fire on lines of trenches.	
11 am do.	MEERUT Divisional Ammunition Column marched for GUARBECQUE in relief to LAHORE Divisional Amn Col.	
11.15 am do.	Telephone message from 2nd Division received that the trench had accomplished the task they had undertaken.	
9 am (about) do.	13th Bde R.H.A. was relieved by 18th Bde R.H.A. of LAHORE Division and marched to ROBECQ.	
11.30 do.	G.O.C. R.A LAHORE Division assumed command of the Artillery on the line from G.O.C R.A. MEERUT Division, who proceeded to LILLERS.	
6 P.M. do.	The position of the MEERUT Divisional Artillery "at rest" is as follows:—	
	G.O.C.R.A. . . . . LILLERS.	
	4th Brigade R.F.A. . . LABASSERIE.	
	9th " " . . . ST FLORIS.	
	13th " " . . . ROBECQ.	
	Divl Amn Col . . . GUARBECQUE.	
	The 110th Heavy Battery remained in action with the LAHORE Division.	

Forms/C. 2118/10

Army Form C. 2118.

WAR DIARY
or
INTELLIGENCE SUMMARY.
(Erase heading not required.)

Instructions regarding War Diaries and Intelligence Summaries are contained in F.S. Regs., Part II. and the Staff Manual respectively. Title pages will be prepared in manuscript.

Hour, Date, Place	Summary of Events and Information	Remarks and references to Appendices
15th February 1915. LILLERS	MEERUT Division resting.	
9 a.m. do	Telephone message received from MEERUT Division stating that information obtained from 2 Alsatian prisoners enemy intended making general attack on 15th/16th.	Appendix 96
3.14 p.m. do	Telephone message from Division stating Major General Anderson proceeding on 10 days leave & that Brig General A.B. Scott would assume command of the Division and Lt Colonel L.A.C. Gordon R.F.A. to command Divisional Artillery during that period.	*Appendix 97 M.Q.D.
16th February 1915. LILLERS	Fine bright day.	
8.6.a.m. do	Telephone message from Division confirming previous intelligence reference general attack by enemy on 15th or 16th.	@ Appendix 98
12 noon do	Brigadier General A.B. Scott attended conference of C.R.A's 1st Army at Indian Corps Headquarters STEVENANT refinery. Artillery observation with aeroplanes.	@ Appendix 99
	Map France 40,000 (BETHUNE) to attached showing positions of Batteries of MEERUT Divisional Artillery at various positions up to about of between 4th February and 13th February 1915. 9lt of Wt plane commencing observations enroute & handing over to LAHORE Divisional Artillery on February 4th also attached.	x Appendix 100 M.Q.D.
17th February 1915 LILLERS	Brigadier General A.B. SCOTT CB. DSO proceeded to Hd Qrs MEERUT Division & assumed command of the Division and Lt Colonel L.A.C. GORDON R.F.A. assumed temporary command of MEERUT Divisional Artillery.	¤ Appendix 101 M.Q.D.

Army Form C. 2118.

WAR DIARY
or
INTELLIGENCE SUMMARY.

(Erase heading not required.)

Instructions regarding War Diaries and Intelligence Summaries are contained in F.S. Regs., Part II. and the Staff Manual respectively. Title pages will be prepared in manuscript.

Hour, Date, Place	Summary of Events and Information	Remarks and references to Appendices
16th February 1915 LILLERS	Telephone message No 289/D/1 from MEERUT Division stating that information has been received from Indian Corps that 44th Howitzer Brigade has been allotted to Indian Corps from 1st Corps, and that one Battery and Brigade Headquarters is allotted to MEERUT Division.	×Appendix 102 M.G.9.
17th February 1915 LILLERS	Brigadier General A.B. SCOTT, C.B. D.S.O proceeded to Headquarters MEERUT Division at BUSNES to take over temporary command of the Division and Lt Colonel L.A.C. GORDON R.F.A. assumed temporary command of MEERUT Divisional Artillery.	M.G.9.
9.15 am. 18th February 1915 LILLERS	MEERUT Division orders. × Telephone message No G 289/D/3 received from MEERUT Division stating it has now been decided that the 43rd How: Brigade will join the Indian Corps, and that 56th Battery will be transferred to 1st Corps. 30th How Battery of 43rd Brigade to join MEERUT Division and been ordered to march to L'ECLEME today.	×Appendix 103
11 a.m. do do	Conference of O.C's R.F.A. Brigades at Headquarters 44th Bde R.F.A. at LA BRASSERIE at which each Brigade was allotted a reconnaissance task to Artillery positions in 3rd, 4th and 5th lines.	
3 P.M. do do	30th How Battery arrived at L'ECLEME.	
7.45 P.M. do do	Information received from LAHORE Divisional Artillery that 30th How Battery should relieve 56th How Battery at 3 P.M tomorrow also that 40th How Battery is to march forward attached to MEERUT Division vice 30th How Battery.	✱ Appendix 104
8 P.M do do	Information received from MEERUT Division that 40th How Battery is marching to L'ECLEME tomorrow.	6 Appendix 101 M.G.9.

Forms/C. 2118/10

Army Form C. 2118.

WAR DIARY
or
INTELLIGENCE SUMMARY.

(Erase heading not required.)

Instructions regarding War Diaries and Intelligence Summaries are contained in F.S. Regs., Part II. and the Staff Manual respectively. Title pages will be prepared in manuscript.

Hour, Date, Place	Summary of Events and Information	Remarks and references to Appendices
19th February 1915. LILLERS	30th How: Battery marched to join LAHORE Divisional Artillery leaving L'ECLEME at 11.30.a.m.	
12 noon do	Lt Colonel LAC GORDON R.F.A. acting C.R.A. accompanied by Brigade Major Q.A. proceeded to BETHUNE to confer with G.O.C. R.A. 2nd Division reference mutual cooperation between the Artillery of the two Divisions when the MEERUT Division again takes over portion of the line.	
2.p.m. do	H0ll How: Battery R.F.A. arrived at L'ECLEME & being temporarily attached to MEERUT Division, vice 30th How: Battery.	MQS
11.a.m. do	114th Heavy Battery arrived in LILLERS for the purpose of changing horses and guns and proceeded and billets at CANTRAINNE.	Appendix 106 MQS
20th February 1915. LILLERS	MEERUT Division Operation Order No 18 dated 20.2.15 relating to relief of LAHORE Division by MEERUT Division on the front line on 21st February 1915 and subsequent days, received.	

Army Form C. 2118.

WAR DIARY
or
INTELLIGENCE SUMMARY.
(Erase heading not required.)

Instructions regarding War Diaries and Intelligence Summaries are contained in F.S. Regs., Part II. and the Staff Manual respectively. Title pages will be prepared in manuscript.

Hour, Date, Place	Summary of Events and Information	Remarks and references to Appendices
21st February 1915 LILLERS	MEERUT Division nohy. Brigadier General R. St C. LECKY, R.A. came to Divisional Artillery Headquarters on his appointment as C.R.A. MEERUT Division. He arrived nas the first intimation of this appointment.	MRO
22nd February 1915 LILLERS	MEERUT Division nohy. During the morning Lt Colonel L.A.C. GORDON, accompanied by Brigadier Major R.A. proceed to LAHORE Divisional Artillery Head Quarters at LOCON to make enquiries with reference to the employment of a detached section at LOISNE and also re the employment of 19th Battery R.F.A. (9th Brigade) in forward position at CROIX BARBEE. This position was also inspected. Official intimation received of appointment of Brigadier General R. St C. LECKY, R.A. as C.R.A. MEERUT Division vice Brigadier General A.B. SCOTT C.B., D.S.O., R.A. appointed C.R.A. Indian Corps. During the day, verbal instructions received from MEERUT Division that on carrying out orders of LAHORE Divisional Artillery the 5th Brigade R.F.A. will not be relieved by the 9th Brigade R.F.A. as had been intended.	Appendix 107
9.30 a.m 23rd February 1915 to LILLERS 5 P.M	G.O.C., R.A. accompanied by Brigade Major R.A. inspected the various Artillery positions to cover the 3rd, 4th and 5th lines which had been previously reconnoitred by the 4th, 9th and 13th Brigades R.F.A.	

Army Form C. 2118.

WAR DIARY
or
INTELLIGENCE SUMMARY.
(Erase heading not required.)

Instructions regarding War Diaries and Intelligence
Summaries are contained in F.S. Regs., Part II.
and the Staff Manual respectively. Title pages
will be prepared in manuscript.

Hour, Date, Place	Summary of Events and Information	Remarks and references to Appendices
5.p.m. 23rd February 1915. LILLERS	G.O.C.R.A. visited G.O.C MEERUT Division at BUSNES and received certain verbal confidential instructions with reference to the reoccupation of the line by the MEERUT Division.	
1.30.p.m. do	Message received from MEERUT Division stating that the 5th Bde R.F.A. (LAHORE Divisional Artillery) will not be relieved to-night.	*Appendix. 108
	Brigadier General R. J. G. LECKY, R.A. took over command of the MEERUT Divisional Artillery during the forenoon, and remained at his post until killed at CHATEAU BLEINY, St QUENTIN N/of AIRE	MCS.
24th February 1915. LILLERS do	MEERUT Division resting.	
7.a.m.	Operation Order No. 10 regarding the relief of the LAHORE Divisional Artillery by the MEERUT Divisional Artillery, issued.	*Appendix. 109
12 noon do	G.O.C.R.A. visited Headquarters 41st Brigade R.F.A. at LA BRASSERIE.	
9.a.m. 25th February 1915. LILLERS	41st Brigade R.F.A. marched from LA BRASSERIE to billets at LA CROIX BAR BEE.	MCS.
11.a.m. do	8th R.F.A. at LA CROIX BAR BEE.	
	G.O.C. R.A. visited Headquarters 13th Brigade R.F.A. and was introduced to the officers of the Brigade.	
11.45.a.m. do	G.O.C.R.A. visited Headquarters 9th Brigade R.F.A. and was introduced to the officers of the Brigade.	

(9/29 6) W 4141—193 100,000 9/14 H W V Forms/C. 2118/10

Army Form C. 2118.

WAR DIARY
or
INTELLIGENCE SUMMARY.
(Erase heading not required.)

Instructions regarding War Diaries and Intelligence
Summaries are contained in F. S. Regs., Part II.
and the Staff Manual respectively. Title pages
will be prepared in manuscript.

Hour, Date, Place	Summary of Events and Information	Remarks and references to Appendices
12.45 p.m. 25th February 1915 LILLERS.	G.O.C. R.A. visited Divisional Ammunition Column and was introduced to officers of that unit.	
4.55 p.m. do	Sanction received from MEERUT Division for move of 9th Bde. to Appendix 110.	
do	R.J.A. from ST FLORIS to billets at LA CROIX MARMEUSE	
5.45 p.m. do	Artillery Reconnaissance Reports for 3rd, 4th & 5th were despatched to MEERUT Division by motor cyclist.	MB23
	Some snow fell during the morning but the weather improved during the day.	
26th February 1915 LOCON. do	Morning opened very misty. observation very difficult till about noon.	
11.35 a.m.	14th Battery fired on gun seen moving close behind the trench in S.5.c. and struck top of parapet with 2nd round	
12 noon do	G.O.C. R.A. MEERUT Division took over command of the artillery on the line from	
12 noon } 1. p.m. } do	G.O.C. R.A. LAHORE Divn. 109th Heavy Battery engaged enemy's battery at S.21.d. 8.2.	
2.10 p.m. do	3rd Siege Battery engaged hostile locality in S.28.a 2.8. with aeroplane observation but unfortunately wireless communication of machine broke down after one round fired	
2.50 p.m. do	Enemy's 5.9" Howitzer Battery started shelling 64th Battery R.F.A. and continued this till about 4.15 p.m. exact location of hostile battery unknown but believed to be battery at T.19.d which was engaged by 110th Heavy Battery with aeroplane observation - range and line obtained but effect not known. The shelling of the 64th Battery by the enemy's 5.9" howitzer was immediately preceded by 4 rounds from PIPSQUEAK battery fired from same locality	
3.30 p.m. do	14th Battery fired on line trenches in S.5.c where Germans seen building obstacles 11 rounds fired and apparently effective	

Forms/C. 2118/10 (3.29.6) W 4141-433 100,000 9/14 H W V

Army Form C. 2118.

WAR DIARY
or
INTELLIGENCE SUMMARY.
(Erase heading not required.)

Instructions regarding War Diaries and Intelligence Summaries are contained in F.S. Regs., Part II. and the Staff Manual respectively. Title pages will be prepared in manuscript.

Hour, Date, Place	Summary of Events and Information	Remarks and references to Appendices
3.40 p.m 26th February 1915 LOCON	2nd Siege Battery again engaged battery in S.28.a.2.8 with aeroplane, which had previously broken down. Line and range given on 5th round. 11 rounds fired for effect.	
5. p.m. Do	4.6 active but then engaged by 110th Heavy Battery it became silent at once. During the day the 4th and 5th Brigades R.F.A. continued registration. The programme arranged with aeroplane for 109th Heavy Battery did not take place owing to wireless communication of machine failing. Hostile guns were not more active this afternoon than some Machine guns behind WHITE House barn were firing a good deal during the morning and evening. The 30th How. Battery registered on SCHOOL House in S.22.a.2.7. The "RITZ" was shelled several times during the day. 8th Siege Battery carried out registration of AUCHY, LA BASSEE Railway Station and AUBERS with wireless aeroplane trenches. The relief of the 11th Bde R.F.A. by the 13th Bde R.F.A was carried out at 11.30. a.m. The relief of the LAHORE Divisional Ammunition Column by the MEERUT Divisional Ammunition Column was also carried out during the forenoon. Intelligence Summary up to 10.p.m 26/2/15 attached as an appx.	WD9

WAR DIARY
or
INTELLIGENCE SUMMARY.
(Erase heading not required.)

Army Form C. 2118.

Instructions regarding War Diaries and Intelligence Summaries are contained in F.S. Regs., Part II. and the Staff Manual respectively. Title pages will be prepared in manuscript.

Hour, Date, Place	Summary of Events and Information	Remarks and references to Appendices
10. 27th February 1915. LOCON	66th Battery fired bursts at WHITE House, suspected of being O.P. 4 hits obtained	
11 a.m. do	RITZ, RUE du BOIS and RICHEBOURG. ST VAAST were shelled by enemy heavy howitzer battery believed to be one that so continuously shelling the RITZ, only moved to another position in S.30 a. 8.4. This battery was engaged by 110th Heavy Battery at intervals during the day. Enemy's light howitzer shelled observing station of 2nd Hv. Battery and again at 1 p.m and 3.15 p.m	
11.20. a.m. do	Reported by O.C. 2nd Siege Battery that Bewry shelled by enemy 5.9" 2 direct hits, and considerable damage done by one - Telephonist wounded badly. 109th Heavy Battery engaged heavy howitzer battery reported by O.C. 110th Heavy Battery about S.30 a. 5.5. Observing Officer reported several rounds falling in hostile battery and one direct hit on a house close by, probably a billet.	
1.25 p.m. do	109th Heavy Battery engaged 4.7 reported by O.C. 5th Bde R.F.A as shelling Bewry.	
1.45 p.m. do	109th Heavy Battery again engaged battery about S.30. a. 5.5 which was reported by observing Officer of 110th Heavy Battery to be shelling the RITZ. Observing Officer 110th Heavy Battery also appeared to think that range and direction was correctly found. Hostile battery (probably No 5) stopped firing during this shoot.	
2.45 p.m. do	2nd Siege Battery fired on S.28 & 3.4. and it did not reply.	
2.55 p.m. do	66th Battery accurately registered one of enemy's machine gun posts - afterwards most effective	

WAR DIARY
or
INTELLIGENCE SUMMARY.
(Erase heading not required.)

Army Form C. 2118.

Hour, Date, Place	Summary of Events and Information	Remarks and references to Appendices
27th February 1915 LOCON 3. p.m.	2nd Siege Battery shelled Scheid near Orchard - pamphlet knocked. After some chevaux de frise and wire entanglements destroyed - H.V. gun (PIPSQUEAK) opened this from close to S.28.8.3.4 - few rounds went over Brewery and later thrown on to LILIAN Village - 2nd Siege Battery got onto him and he stopped. 73rd Battery fired four rounds at horses in RUE du MARAIS and QUINQUE RUE which were inspected & hers O.P.'s of hostile battery firing on Brewery.	
do. 3.15 p.m.	11th Heavy Battery fired on LORGIES in response to shelling of RICHEBOURG ST VAAST, the hostile battery doing this was undoubtedly T19Z.	
do. 3.40 p.m.	One gun (6") 8th Siege Battery fired on LORGIES in response to hostile shelling of RICHEBOURG. See Intelligence Summary up to 11 p.m. 27.2.15 - attached to an appx	MW2.
28th February 1915. LOCON 6.40. a.m.	Very clear morning, with high wind blowing. 14th Battery fired 2 effective rounds on party crossing barricade in S.5.C.3.4	
7.20 am	66th Battery shelled, with some effect, Redoubt in S.10.d. no several persons seen in Redoubt also much movement there.	
7.45.a.7.	14th Battery fired at working party behind fire trench in S.5.C - 4 hits on parapet, where there had been considerable activity during past 3 days.	

Army Form C. 2118.

WAR DIARY
or
INTELLIGENCE SUMMARY.
(Erase heading not required.)

Instructions regarding War Diaries and Intelligence
Summaries are contained in F. S. Regs., Part II.
and the Staff Manual respectively. Title pages
will be prepared in manuscript.

Hour, Date, Place	Summary of Events and Information	Remarks and references to Appendices
8.a.m. 28th February 1915 LOCON	114th Battery ranged on house S.5.d.5.7 - probable O.P. covered in car seen to destroy it.	
9.a.m. do	114th Battery fired at barricade across road at S.11.a	
9.45 a.m. do	8th Siege Battery registered on LORGIES with aerial observation.	
10.a.m. do	G.O.C., R.A. accompanied G.O.C. MEERUT Division and reconnoitred certain Artillery positions in the neighbourhood of RICHEBOURG. ST VAAST	
10.20.a.m. do	114th Battery shelled O.P. in N-A.5.7 - 2 direct hits on house	
11.44 a.m. do	114th Battery fired at snipers in the trenches in S.11.a	
12. noon do	66th Battery fired a few rounds at German flag at corner of plantation. S.10.e.	
	114th Battery fired 2 rounds at Salient near orchard.	
2.15 p.m. do	8th Siege Battery engaged 15.c.m Howitzer at T.19.a 0.2, with visual observation from RUE du BOIS - 3 rounds reported burst + line.	
3.15 p.m. do	Mobile batteries in S.28 & 3.4. & opened fire on house B - below an arrangement being made to/the/battery to bombard Salient near Orchard in any way with 73rd Battery R.F.A. O.C. of these Batteries communicated with 35th H. B. who wanted a target - observing officer 2/Lieut got 35 Heavy Battery on to this - effect good	
3.45 p.m. do	8th Siege Battery obtained range on a battery at S.28.b 3.4, with aerial observation.	
4.30 p.m. do	G.O.C. R.A. visited G.O.C. R.A. 8th Division with reference to mutual cooperation.	

Army Form C. 2118.

WAR DIARY
or
INTELLIGENCE SUMMARY.
(Erase heading not required.)

Instructions regarding War Diaries and Intelligence Summaries are contained in F.S. Regs., Part II. and the Staff Manual respectively. Title pages will be prepared in manuscript.

Hour, Date, Place	Summary of Events and Information	Remarks and references to Appendices
4.45 p.m. 28th February 1915. LOCON	The Rebels in S 10 d caught fire and burnt for some time.	M.E.
5. p.m. do	73rd Battery fired a few rounds at a house in the RUE du MARAIS, outside which some flag signallers were seen. Also see Intelligence Summary up to 11.P.M 28/2/15 attached as an appendix.	

1st March 1915

W.W. Shepherd-Saunder
Major R.A.
Brigade Major, Royal Artillery
Meerut Division

APPENDIX 86

Extract from 1st Corps Operation Order No.65,
dated 30/1/15.

x　　x　　x　　x　　x　　x

2. (a) The 110th and 114th Heavy Batteries R.G.A. and the
2nd and 8th Siege Batteries R.G.A. will remain in their
present positions and come under the Indian Corps for all
purposes from the 3rd February inclusive.

(b) The 113th Heavy Battery R.G.A. now attached to the 1st
Division will be transferred to the Indian Corps Area and
come under the Indian Corps for all purposes on a date to
be fixed later.

(c) The 26th Heavy Battery R.G.A. will remain in its
present position and eventually come under the orders of
the 2nd Division.

(d) The 44th Bde R.F.A. (how) will be transferred to the
positions now occupied by the 43rd Bde R.F.A. (how) under
arrangements between 1st and 2nd Divisions, and the 43rd
Bde R.F.A. (how) will then be temporarily attached to
the Indian Corps.

(e) The remaining F.A. Bdes of the 2nd Division will be
relieved by the F.A. Bdes of the Indian Corps beginning
on the 3rd February.

(f) The relief of the remaining F.A. Bdes of the 1st
Division by those of the 2nd Division will be arranged
between the Commanders of these Divisions as may be most
convenient.

x　　x　　x　　x　　x　　x

No. 255/21-G.

The C.R.A.

The units which are shown in the above extract order
as coming under the Indian Corps will be attached to the
MEERUT Division.

Please arrange, in direct communication with the C.R.A.
2nd Division, for the reliefs to be given effect to.

~~Operation Orders will follow in due course.~~

Crowe,
Lieutenant-Colonel,
General Staff, MEERUT Division.

31-1-1915.

Copy to :-
"A" Branch
"Q"   "

APPENDIX 87   Copy No. 28

OPERATION ORDERS No. 2
by
Lieut Colonel L.A.C. GORDON, Royal Field Artillery
Commanding Royal Artillery, MEERUT Division.

Reference:-
Map- FRANCE,(BETHUNE) 1/40,000   H A M.   1st February 1915.
and,
ARRAS sheet 1/80,000

1. **INTENTION.** The MEERUT Divisional Artillery will relieve the 2nd Divisional Artillery on 3rd and 4th February.

2. **GROUPING.** The 4th Brigade R.F.A.(less one battery) and 13th Brigade R.F.A.(less one battery) will relieve the 36th and 34th Brigades R.F.A. on 3rd and 4th February, respectively.   These two brigades under the command of Lieut Colonel L.A.C. GORDON, R.F.A. will be grouped with the DEHRA DUN Brigade.
The 9th Brigade R.F.A.(less one battery) will relieve the 41st Brigade R.F.A. on the 4th February. It will be grouped with the BAREILLY Brigade, and will be under the command of Lieut Colonel F. POTTS, R.F.A. who will also have 2 howitzer batteries (Nos. 37 and   ) under his command.

3. **RESERVE Batteries.** One Reserve Battery per Brigade will proceed into billets near LA GIX HARMEUSE which will be indicated by the Staff Captain, Royal Artillery.

4. **DIVISIONAL ARTILLERY and AMMUNITION COLUMN.** The 35th, 110th and 114th Heavy Batteries and 2nd and 8th Siege Batteries will come under the immediate orders of the G.O.C., R.A., MEERUT Division from the time he assumes command of the Divisional Artillery.
The Divisional Ammunition Column will be established in the neighbourhood of PARADIS and will take up supply of ammunition from 12 noon 4th February 1915.

5. **BRIGADE AMMUNITION SUPPLY.** The 4th and 13th Brigade Ammunition Columns at LES LOBES will supply 18 pr. ammunition to their own Brigades.   The 4th Brigade Ammunition Column will supply S.A.A. to the DEHRA DUN Brigade.
The 13th Brigade Ammunition Column will supply S.A.A. to the Infantry Brigade in Divisional Reserve, and Divisional Troops.
The 9th Brigade Ammunition Column at LE CASSAN will supply 18 pr. ammunition to its own Brigade and S.A.A. to the BAREILLY Brigade.
Supply of ammunition will in all cases commence from 12 noon on date of relief.
Howitzer Brigade Ammunition Column is established at LES LOBES.

6. **MOVEMENTS.** Will be carried out in accordance with attached March Table.

7. **TELEPHONIC COMMUNICATION** Existing wire will be taken over as it now stands. Brigade Commanders will see that the same amount of wire is handed back to the 2nd Divisional Artillery as was received by them in December 1914.

8. **SUPPLIES.** All units will refill at BOURECQ on the 3rd February and at LOCON on the 4th February.

9.	RAILHEADS.	SUPPLIES............LILLERS.
		AMMUNITION.........St VENANT.
10.	COMMAND.	The G.O.C., R.A. MEERUT Division will assume command from the C.R.A. 2nd Division after completion of reliefs on the 4th February.
11.	REPORTS.	Reports to LOCON.
12.	ROUTINE & STANDING ORDERS.	Special attention is invited to the orders on "Settlement of claims", "Billets being left clean" and "March discipline".

(signature)
Major R.A.
Brigade Major, Royal Artillery,
MEERUT DIVISION.

Issued at 6.p.m.
By mounted orderly.

Copies to :-

```
        No.1..............to General Staff, MEERUT Division.
        No.2..............to G.O.C. MEERUT Detachment.
        No.3..............to G.O.C. DEHRA DUN Brigade.
        No.4..............to G.O.C. BAREILLY Brigade.
        No.5..............to C.R.A., 2nd Division.
        Nos.6 to 10.......to O.C. 4th Brigade R.F.A.
        Nos.11 to 15......to O.C. 9th Brigade R.F.A.
        Nos.16 to 20......to O.C. 13th Brigade R.F.A.
        Nos.21............to O.C. Meerut Divisional Ammunition Column
        No.22.............to O.C. No.35 Heavy Battery R.G.A.
        No.23.............to O.C. No.110 Heavy Battery R.G.A.
        No.24.............to O.C. 114th Heavy Battery R.G.A.
        No.25.............to O.C. 2nd Siege Battery R.G.A.
        No.26.............to O.C. 8th Siege Battery R.G.A.
        No.27.............to O.C. 37th How: Battery R.F.A.
        No.28.............to WAR DIARY.
```

MARCH TABLE.

MEERUT DIVISIONAL ARTILLERY.

(Reference paragraph 6 Operation Order No.8 dated 1st February 1915).

Date.	Unit.	Time of start	From.	To.	Time of arrival	Remarks.
3.2.15.	4th Bde Ammunition Column	8.a.m.	LIERES	LES LOBES	12 noon.	To relieve 36th Bde Ammunition Column by 12 noon. Via LILLERS, CHOCQUES, HINGES and LOCON.
3.2.15.	4th Bde R.F.A.(less one battery)	8.a.m.	LIERES	LA COUTURE	1.30 p.m.	To relieve 36th Bde R.F.A. by 2.p.m. (Same route as above).
3.2.15.	66th Battery R.F.A.	...	LIERES	LA CIX MARMEUSE	...	To billets. (Same route as above).
3.2.15.	Meerut Divisional Amm Column.	8.a.m.	NEDON-CHELLE	PARADIS	...	ANETTES, LILLERS, CHOCQUES and HINGES. Commence ammunition supply at 12 noon on 4th February 1915.
4.2.15.	9th Bde Ammunition Column.	8.a.m.		LE CASSAN	12 noon	Via CHOCQUES, BETHUNE and ESSARS.
4.2.15.	9th Bde R.F.A.(less one battery)	8.a.m.	FERFAY	LE TOURET	1.30 p.m.	To relieve 41st Bde R.F.A. by 2.p.m. Via CHOCQUES, BETHUNE and ESSARS.
4.2.15.	19th Battery R.F.A.	8.a.m.	FERFAY	LA CIX MARMEUSE	...	To billets. Via CHOCQUES, BETHUNE and LOCON.
4.2.15.	13th Bde Ammunition Column.	8.a.m.	LA LOTERIE	LES LOBES	12 noon	To relieve 34th Bde Ammunition Column by 12 noon. Via ROBECQ, HINGES and LOCON.
4.2.15.	13th Bde R.F.A.(less one battery)	8.a.m.	LA LOTERIE	LA COUTURE	1.30 p.m.	To relieve 34th Bde R.F.A. by 2.p.m. Via ROBECQ, HINGES and LOCON.
4.2.15.	8th Battery R.F.A.	8.a.m.	LA LOTERIE	LA CIX MARMEUSE	...	To billets. Via ROBECQ, HINGES and LOCON.

Notes:- (1) Time of starting from billets fixed by MEERUT Division is 8.a.m. but application has been made to the Corps that units may start at 6.a.m.
(2) The 4th and 9th Brigade Ammunition Columns must be prepared to supply all ammunition and 13th Brigade Ammunition Column to supply gun ammunition by 12 noon on day of relief.

[signature]
Capt. R.A.,
Brigade Major, Royal Artillery,
MEERUT DIVISION.

2nd February 1915.

"A" Form. Army Form C. 2121.
MESSAGES AND SIGNALS.

APPENDIX 88

TO — C R A   H A M

* G 453/1   1st   Ras 5"5"   AAA

Indian corps 9307 begins place 37th Howitzer battery at disposal of Meerut divn AAA Battery commdr to report to Meerut divn at Zoon tomorrow at eleven am addressed Lahore repeated Meerut divn ref his G 9253/24 ends for information.

From: MEERUT DIVN
Time: 10.55 PM

"A" Form. Army Form C. 2121.

MESSAGES AND SIGNALS.

APPENDIX 89

TO — C R A Meerut

Sender's Number: G253/37
Day of Month: 2nd
In reply to Number: —
AAA

Continuation my G253/34 Indian Corps wire begins G348 2nd my G308 dated 1st AAA 1st Corps agrees to routes and will keep them open ends AAA G308 communicated to you in my G253/32

Place: Meerut Division

APPENDIX 90
5

Copy No. ....

Operation Order No. 15.
By
Lieutenant-General C.A.Anderson, C.B., Commanding Meerut Division.

Lillers, 1st February 1915.

Reference - Map France (Bethune) 1/40,000.

Intention.	1.	The Meerut Division will take over a portion of the trenches now held by the 2nd Division, in addition to the portion now held by the Meerut Detachment, on the night of 1st/2nd February.
Dehra Dun Bde.	2.	The Dehra Dun Brigade will remain in occupation of its present trenches.
Bareilly Bde.	3.	The Bareilly Brigade will take over the front now held by the 6th Infy. Bde. Details of the relief will be arranged by the Brigadiers concerned.
Garhwal Bde.	4.	The Garhwal Brigade will form the Divisional reserve, and will remain in its present billets.
Royal Arty.	5.	The relief of the 2nd Divisional Artillery by the Meerut Divisional Artillery will begin on the 3rd instant, and will be carried out by the Brigadiers concerned.
4th Ind. Cavy.	6.	The 4th Ind. Cavy. will march to billets near LE VERTBOIS FE on the morning of the 2nd February. Route :- LILLERS - L'ECLEME - ROBECQ.
Supplies.	7.	Units will refill supplies at the same time and places as today, with the following exceptions :-

4th Seaforths refill with Dehra Dun Bde. At ZELOBES at 10.15 a.m.
No. 4 Coy. S. & Ms.
Divl. Headquarters   Refill at LOCON at 10 a.m.
Divl. R.E. Headquarters

Reports.   8. The G. O. C., Meerut Division will assume command of the line held by the Division at 10 a.m. on February 2nd. Reports to Meerut Division Headquarters, LOCON, after that hour.

Crorie

Lieutenant-Colonel,
General Staff, Meerut Division.

Issued at 4.30 p.m.
by Signal Company, to :-

Copy No. 1 - Indian Corps   Copy No. 10)
          2 - Dehra Dun Bde.   11)
          3 - Garhwal Bde.   12 } A. Q. M. G.
          4 - Bareilly Bde.   13)
          5 - G.R.A.   14)
          6 - G.R.E.   15 - 1st Corps.
          7 - 4th Ind. Cavy.   16 - 2nd Division
          8 - 107th Pioneers   17 - Meerut Detachment.
          9 - Meerut Sig. Coy.   18)
                                              19 } War Diary and file
                                              20)

"A" Form.　Army Form C. 2121.

MESSAGES AND SIGNALS.

	Words	Charge	APPENDIX 41	Recd. at 9.27 a.m.
Service Instructions	43		This message is on a/c of 98 Service.	Date 5.2.15
	Sent At ___ m. To ___ By ___		(Signature of "Franking Officer.")	From SCO By Johnston

TO: RA Meerut Divn

Sender's Number	Day of Month	In reply to Number	AAA
BM 67	4th		

2nd. Div Arty who take over from us before relief of 113th hy bty wish one section each of 35th and 113th to exchange on 8th and other on 9th as in programme

5ᵃ

From 1st RA.
Place
Time 8.0 am

The above may be forwarded as now corrected. (Z)

"A" Form.   Army Form C. 2121.
MESSAGES AND SIGNALS.

APPENDIX 92

PRIORITY

TO — C.R.A.
Meerut

Sender's Number: G 264/1
Day of Month: 5th

First Corps wires begins following wire received from Army begins 18pr Anti aircraft gun to be sent immediately to report to 2nd Corps HQ at BAILLEUL aaa it is to be placed at disposal of 2nd Army at once aaa Wire to second Corps direct probable time of arrival at BAILLEUL ends please issue necessary orders and wire me probable hour of arrival BAILLEUL Addressed Meerut Divn repeated 1st Corps AAA Please issue necessary orders and furnish me with information required

From / Place: Meerut Divn
Time: 11-5 AM

Amendment to Meerut Divn Operation Order No.17 of 6/2/15

Column 6 of March Table, opposite "No.3 Coy S. & M." in Column 2, for "20th" read "21st".

Davies

Major,
General Staff.

Meerut Divn.
7/2/15.

APPENDIX 92a

Copy No. 5

OPERATION ORDER No. 17.
By
LIEUTENANT GENERAL C.A. ANDERSON, C.B.,
COMMANDING MEERUT DIVISION.

LOCON,
Reference Map:-   6th February 1915.
FRANCE - BETHUNE Sheet 1:40,000.

Intention. 1. The MEERUT Division will be relieved in the front line by the LAHORE Division on the 8th February and subsequent days.

Movements. 2. Moves of the Infantry Brigades and Divisional Troops will be as in the attached march table.

Infantry Reliefs. 3. Reliefs of troops in the trenches will be carried out by the Brigadiers concerned in direct communication with each other.

The G.O.s C. Bareilly and Garhwal Brigades will remain in command of their respective portions of the line until the relief of their troops has been completed, when the command will be assumed by the G.O.s C. Sirhind and Jullundur Brigades respectively. Hour of handing over and assuming command to be immediately reported to Divnl: H. Q.

Artillery. 4. The artillery of the Meerut Division will be relieved by that of the Lahore Division on 13th and 14th February under arrangements to be mutually agreed on by the C.R.A.s Lahore and Meerut Divisions.

S. & M. 5. Details of relief of S. & M. Companies will be arranged by the C.R.E.s Lahore and Meerut Divisions.

Garhwal Brigade Lahore Div. Reserve. 6. The Garhwal Brigade will remain at LA COUTURE at the disposal of the G.O.C. Lahore Division as Divisional Reserve.

Ambulances. 7. Details of relief of Field Ambulances will be arranged by the A.D.s M.S. Lahore and Meerut Divisions.
No. 129 I.F.A. will remain at PARADIS.

Trench Guns. 8. All trench guns and ammunition will be handed over to the incoming Brigades.

Supplies. 9. (a) Units will refill supplies at their present refilling points on day of marching, with the exception of the artillery units relieved on 14th instant, and the 19th B.F.A. & 128th I.F.A. which will refill in new area on day of marching.

Gum boots. (b) All gum boots in possession of units, including those lent by the Jullundur Brigade, will be handed over to the relieving Brigades. Brigadiers will report the numbers handed over.

Braziers. (c) All braziers in the front line will be handed over to the relieving Brigades. Brigadiers will report the approximate numbers handed over.

Commands. 10. G.O.C. Meerut Divn will remain in command of the line till ten a.m. on the 12th February when command of the front area will be handed over to the G.O.C. Lahore Divn.

Reports. 11. Meerut Divn H.Q. will open at CHATEAU BUSNES at ten a.m. on 12th February.

Issued at 6.0 P.M. by Signal Coy.,

Lt. Colonel,
General Staff, MEERUT DIVISION.

Copy No. 1 to Indian Corps,
    2   Dehra Dun Bde
    3   Garhwal Bde   Copy No. 9 to Meerut Sig. Coy.
    4   Bareilly Bde   10   A.Q.M.G.
    5   C.R.A. Meerut Div.   11   D.A.A.G.
    6   C.R.E. do.   12   D.A.A. & Q.M.G. (Thro' A.Q.M.G.)
    7   4th Ind. Cavalry.   13   A.D.M.S.
    8   107th Ind. Pioneers. 14   Train
   15   2nd Divn   16   8th Division   17   Lahore Divn.
18, 19 & 20   War Diary & files.

P.T.O.

M A R C H   T A B L E.

Date.	Unit.	From.	to.	via	Remarks.
1	2	3	4	5	6
Feby 8th	Dehra Dun Brigade	LA COUTURE	CALONNE and area S.W. of that place.	FOSSE – LA CROIX MARMEUSE – LE CORNET MALO.	To march on arrival of Sirhind Bde at 11.0 A.M.
do.	No.2 Coy. Train	FOSSE	Billets S.W. of CALONNE	do.	Baggage section to follow Brigade.
9th	Bareilly Brigade	Trenches	LA COUTURE and VIELLE CHAPELLE.		After relief by Sirhind Bde. on afternoon & evening 9th.
do.	19 B.F.A.	ZELOBES	CALONNE	) LA CROIX MARMEUSE–	
do.	128 I.F.A.	VIELLE CHAPELLE	LES RUES DES VACHES.	) LE CORNET MALO	
10th	Bareilly Brigade	LA COUTURE & VIELLE CHAPELLE	CALONNE & area N.W. of that place.	(FOSSE – ½mile South of LESTREM – LE Gd PACAUT.	To march on arrival of JULLUNDUR Bde at 11.0 A.M.
do.	No.4 Coy Train	CORNET MALO	CALONNE (Mill)	do. do.	Baggage Sect to follow Bde
do.	107th Ind Pioneers	PICHBOURG St. VAAST & MESCLAUX	ROBECQ (N.E.)	LOCON – HINGETTE	The ½ battn at RICHEBOURG will be moved to MESPLAUX on 9th under separate order.
do.	20 B.F.A.	XXXXXX LOCON	St. FLORIS	) FOSSE – ½mile S. of	
do.	130 ¾.F.A.	LOCON	CALONNE	) LESTREM – Le Gd PACAUT.	
11th	Garhwal Bde	Trenches	LACOUTURE & VIELLE CHAPELLE		On relief by JULLUNDUR Bde on afternoon & evening 11th.
do.	No.4 Coy S. & H.	LE TOURET	CALONNE (S.E.)	(FOSSE – Le Cix MARMEUSE Le CORNET MALO	To billets vacated by 20th Coy S. & H.
12th	4th Ind Cavalry	LESLOBE	HAMLET BILLET	Will be notified later	To billets vacated by 15thHrs
13th	No.3 Coy S. & H.	Richebourg St.VAAST	St. FLORIS	FOSSE – ½mile S.LESTREM	To billets vacated by 20th Coy S. & M.
No. do.	No.1 Coy Train	CORNET MALO	Billets N.W.of ROBECQ.) LOCON-LESLOBE-road jn		Baggage wagons to march independently with their own units
Do.	H.Q. Mule Transport	do.	MARQUOIS	(Q.28.d –RIEZ du VINAGE–	
12th	Divn H. Q.	LOCON	BUSNES	) DOUCE CREME Fe.	

MESSAGES AND SIGNALS.

"A" Form.   Army Form C. 2121.

APPENDIX 93

TO: C.R.A   "A" Branch / Q Branch

Sender's Number: G 275/3   Day of Month: 9th   AAA

Indian Corps wire begins 0457 9th Fifth Corps ask 114 Heavy Battery and 37th Howitzer Battery to join on twelfth AAA Destination not yet given but asked for AAA Give batteries and their ammunition columns as preliminary warning AAA Addressed Meerut and Lahore Divisions ends for information in continuation my G 275/1

From Place: Meerut Division

No. 213 RA(L).   9/2/15.

O.C. 37th How: Battery R.F.A.
114th Heavy Battery R.G.A.

Indian Corps wires begins 0457 9th Fifth Corps ask 114 Heavy Battery and 37th How: Battery to join on twelfth AAA Destination not yet given but asked for AAA Give batteries and their Ammunition Columns preliminary warning AAA addressed Meerut and Lahore Divisions ends for information.

2. Please inform your Ammunition Column.
3. O.C. 37th How. Battery to inform O.C. 9th Bde R.F.A.

J.M. Lynch-Staunton
Major R.A.
Brigade Major R.A.
Meerut Division

MESSAGES AND SIGNALS.

TO: CRA — Q Branch / A Branch

Sender's Number: G275/4   Day of Month: 9th   In reply to Number: —   AAA

Indian Corps now notify that as guns of 114th Heavy Battery condemned and fifth Corps have no means of remounting new guns 113th Heavy battery will be sent instead of 114th as arranged in correspondence ending with my No. G275/3 today

Place: MEERUT DIVISION
Time: 6 pm

N: 216 R A (L).   9/2/15.   89

Copy of memo from Brigade Major R.A. Meerut Division to O.C's 37th How Battery R.F.A and 114th Heavy Bty R.G.A No 213 RA(L) of 9/2/15

Indian Corps wires begins 0457 9th Infth Corps ask 114 Heavy Battery and 37th How Battery to join on civilight AAA Destination not yet given but asked for AAA Give batteries and their Ammunition Columns preliminary warning AAA addressed Meerut and Lahore Divisions ends for information. —
2. Please inform your Ammunition Column
3. O.C. 37th How Bty to join O.C 9th Bde R.F.A

O.C. 113th Heavy Battery R.G.A

Indian Corps now wires that as guns of 114th are in lorries and 5th Corps have no means of mounting waggons 113th Heavy Battery will be sent instead of 114th Heavy Battery —

Please acknowledge —

C.G. Robinson   Captain RA
                        for Major R.A.
                   Meerut Division.

Copies to :- O.C. 114th Heavy Battery
             O.C. 37th How Battery

"A" Form.   Army Form
MESSAGES AND SIGNALS.

APPENDIX 94

TO — CRA

Sender's Number	Day of Month	In reply to Number	
G 275/5	10th		AAA

My G 275/3 and G 275/4 AAA Indian Corps wires begins 37th How and 113th Heavy batteries accompanied by sections Ammn Cols will march tomorrow on transfer to fifth Corps AAA following is route arranged AAA LA GORGUE NEUF BERQUIN — VIEUX BERQUIN — STRAZEELE to CAESTRE where they will billet night eleventh twelfth making their own arrangements AAA Thence on twelfth via STEENVOORDE and POPERINGHE to destination at BRANDHOEK LEMAN 2½ miles due East of POPERINGHE ends Please issue necessary orders

145

From: Meerut Divn
Place:
Time: 1-30 P.M

Lt Col
G.S.O.(1)

Copy No. 24

OPERATION ORDER No.
by
Brigadier General A.B. SCOTT, C.B., D.S.O.,
Commanding Royal Artillery, MEERUT Division.

APPENDIX 95

Reference:— 1
((BRENDE, BETHUNE) 40,000
Map (and   1
(ARRAS Sheet 80,000

L O C O N , 10th February 1915.

INTENTION.	1.	With reference to paragraph 4 of MEERUT Division Operation Order No.17 dated the 8th February 1915, the MEERUT Divisional Artillery will be relieved as follows:—

13th   (6th Brigade R.F.A. by 5th Brigade R.F.A.
February   (4th Brigade R.F.A. by 11th Brigade R.F.A.

14th   ((13th Brigade R.F.A. by 18th Brigade R.F.A.
February   (Divisional Ammunition Column.

Hour of relief is fixed for 12 noon. After this hour reliefs will take place as favourable opportunities occur by Brigade and Battery Commanders concerned working in direct communication with each other.

MOVEMENTS.   2. Routes to billets and times of starting are given in the accompanying March Table.

TELEPHONIC   3. Existing wire will be handed over to incoming units as it
COMMUNICATION   now stands. Units will receive the equivalent amount from LAHORE Divisional Artillery that they handed over to 2nd Divisional Artillery.

SUPPLIES.   4. Units being relieved will refill in accordance with MEERUT Division memo No.Q-5/17 of to-day's date. Times for refilling are, however, altered as follows:—
LOCON at 8.30.a.m.
Cross roads R.C.C. at 8.45.a.m.
On the 14th instant units will refill as follows:—
  4th Brigade R.F.A.   )
  Meerut Div'l Ammunition Col.) POBECQ 10.a.m.
  6th Brigade R.F.A. CALONNE Q.S.R. 10.a.m.
  13th Brigade R.F.A. CALONNE Q.S.R. 10.a.m.
  55th How: Battery R.F.A.   ) Cross roads R.C.C.
  110th Heavy Battery R.G.A.) at 8.45.a.m.

RAILHEAD.   5.   SUPPLIES............LILLERS.
                  AMMUNITION..........ST VENANT.

COMMAND.   6. The G.O.C., R.A. MEERUT Division will remain in command of the Artillery on the line until 12 noon on 14th February, when command of the Artillery will be handed over to the G.O.C., R.A. LAHORE Division.

REPORTS,   7. MEERUT Divisional Artillery Headquarters will open at Main Square in L I L L E R S
at 12 noon on the 14th February 1915.

ROUTINE &   8. Special attention is again invited to the orders on
STANDING   "Settlement of claims", "Billets being left clean", "March
ORDERS.   Discipline", also to MEERUT Division, General Staff Memo-
                randum No.G-258/10 dated the 8th February 1915. Routes
                mentioned in the March Table should be thoroughly
                reconnoitred beforehand.

Major R.A.

Issued at ?.D.S   Brigade Major, Royal Artillery,
By mounted orderly.   MEERUT DIVISION.
Copies to:—
No.1 to General Staff, Meerut Division.   No.19 to O.C. 110th (H) Battery.
No.2 to G.O.C., R.A. LAHORE Division.   No.20 to O.C. 114th   do.
Nos.3 to 7 to O.C. 4th Bde R.F.A.   No.21 to O.C. 2nd Siege Battery.
Nos.8 to 12 to O.C. 6th Bde R.F.A.   No.22 to O.C. 6th Siege Battery.
Nos.13 to 17 to O.C. 13th Bde R.F.A.   No.23 to O.C. 55th How: Bty R.F.A.
No.18 to O.C. Meerut Div'l Ammn Col.   No.24 to WAR DIARY.

References:-
FRANCE 1
(BETHUNE) 40,000

MARCH TABLE
MEERUT DIVISIONAL ARTILLERY

Date	Unit	Station at	To	Time	Route and Remarks
13.2.15.	9th Bde R.F.A (less one battery)	RUE des CHAVATTES	St FLORIS (P.6.a.)	on relief after 12 noon	Le TOURET-LA COUTURE FOSSE-Cix MARMEUSE PACAUT-QUENTIN CALONNE-St FLORIS One battery from Cix MARMEUSE.
13.2.15.	9th Brigade Ammunition Column	Le CASSAN	St FLORIS (P.6.a.)	on relief after 12 noon	LOCON-CORNET MALO (W.6.d.) PACAUT-St FLORIS.
13.2.15.	4th Brigade R.F.A.(less one battery)	CROIX-BARBEE	LA BRASSERIE (P.21.d.)	on relief after 12 noon	Road junction(M.20. C.1.8) Road junction (R.28.d.) FOSSE Cix MARMEUSE-LE CORNET MALO(Q.28.a) Pt LEVIS(Q.32.a.) Mt BERNENCHON ROBECQ-LA BRASSERIE. One battery from Cix MARMEUSE.
13.2.15.	4th Brigade Ammunition Column	ZELOBES	LA BRASSERIE	x 8.a.m.	LE CORNET MALO(Q.28.a as above to LA BRASSERIE.
14.2.15.	13th Bde R.F.A.(less one battery)	RUE des CHAVATTES	ROBECQ	on relief after 12 noon.	LE TOURET-ESSARS-BETHUNE-Mt BERNENCHON ROBECQ
14.2.15.	One Battery 13th Bde R.F.A.	Cix MARMEUSE	ROBECQ	8.a.m.	As 4th Bde R.F.A. route. To be clear of cross roads Q.27.a. by 9.30.a.m.
14.2.15.	13th Bde Ammunition Column	LES LOBES	ROBECQ	ø 8.a.m.	LE CORNET MALO(Q.28.a and 4th Bde R.F.A. route. To follow battery 13th Bde and be clear of cross roads Q.27.a. by 10.a.m.
14.2.15.	Divisional Ammunition Column	PARADIS	GUARBECQUE	3 Sections at 8.a.m. one section on relief after 12 noon.	HINGES-GONNEHEIM BUSNETTES-BUSNES GUARBECQUE.

Notes:- x Ammunition Supply of troops in Northern Section will be taken up by 13th Brigade Ammunition Column at LES LOBES till arrival of 11th Brigade Ammunition Column at noon.

ø Ammunition supply of troops in Northern Section will be taken up by 11th Brigade Ammunition Column at ZELOBES till arrival of 13th Brigade Ammunition Column at noon.

Meerut Div RA

APPENDIX 95a

B.M. 582. 13th.

SECRET.

The French intend to advance their left wing tomorrow the 14th in A 21 b & d. The 4th Brigade will also adjust their right front line to conform. The movement will be made at 10.5 a.m.

2. The 2nd Divisional Artillery will co-operate by keeping up fire at a rapid rate from 10 to 10.5 and at a moderate rate until the situation is secured.

3. The Artillery taking part and objectives and rounds allotted are as follows:-

41st Brigade.) As arranged in consultation between
required rounds as ~~received~~.) O.C. 41st F.A. Brigade and G.O.C.4th
1st Siege Bty..) Guards Brigade. But no fire is to
15 rounds per gun.) be directed W. of a line running
N. & S. through cross roads A 22 a
1.6 after 10.5 a.m.

60th battery will only be used in case of emergency.
26th. Heavy Battery.. AUCHY. Rounds as required.
35th. Heavy Battery.. S.W. Face of Triangle.
    Rounds as required.
Armoured Train.. Triangle and Canal Bank.
    Rounds as required.

4. In the event of hostile guns opening fire they will be dealt with as under.

AUCHY neighbourhood - 26th Heavy Battery.
VIOLAINES.. - 35th Heavy Battery.
LA BASSEE.. - Armoured Train.

5. The French Artillery will deal with guns and trenches South of the LA BASSEE road (except AUCHY) and with LA BASSEE road itself, and will also direct enfilade fire across the trenches W. of Triangle.
The Meerut Artillery is co-operating by firing on TRIANGLE and on CANTELEUX and guns to the northwards.

6. All observers will keep a close watch on their own fronts for any movement.

7. Communication with the French will be maintained through Headquarters and through an officer of the 26th Heavy Battery who will be stationed on the CINDER HEAP at ANNEQUIN, where a representative of the French Artillery will be.

8. Correct time will be obtained from Signals.

Acknowledge.

R.A. 2nd Div. Captain R.A.
8.p.m. Brigade Major R.A. 2nd Division
Addressed 34th,36th,41st,44th Bdes,26th and 35th Heavy,
1st Siege, 8th Siege Btys, Armoured Train. Repeated 2nd Div.
4th Guards Bde.& Meerut R.A.

"A" Form. Army Form C. 2121.

MESSAGES AND SIGNALS.

No. of Message _____

Prefix _____ Code _____ m. | Words | Charge | APPENDIX 96
Office of Origin and Service Instructions. | | | This message is on a/c of : | Recd. at _____ m.
| Sent | | Date F I G
At _____ m. | | Service | 15-2-15
To _____ | | | From _____
By _____ | | (Signature of "Franking Officer.") | By L' Richmond

TO { C R A

Sender's Number | Day of Month | In reply to Number | AAA
IG 34/1 | 15th | |

First army wires that French
ninth Corps states that two
ALSATIANS who came today
to French lines being cross-
examined separately both
state that enemy intended
to deliver a general
attack on 15th or 16th
addressed CRA CRE 4th
Cavalry 107th Pioneers DEHRA
DUN BDE repeated BAREILLY
BDE for information
reference + 243/IG of eighth

From MEERUT DIVN
Place
Time 9 A M

MESSAGES AND SIGNALS.				No. of Message
Prefix ___ Code ___ m. Office of Origin and Service Instructions.	Words 50	Charge	APPENDIX 91 This message is on a/c of:	Recd. at 3.14 p m.
	Sent At ___ m. To ___ By ___		Service (Signature of "Franking Officer.")	Date 15-2-15 From YIG By R Richmond

TO Genl Scott CRA

Sender's Number	Day of Month	In reply to Number	AAA
A293/127	15th		

Genl ANDERSON has been granted ten days leave aaa He proceeds at 10.45 am 16th inst aaa You will officiate in command of the divn and Lieut-Col L A C GORDON 4th Bde RFA will officiate in command of Divnl Arty

From MEERUT DIVN

Place

Time

MESSAGES AND SIGNALS.

"A" Form. Army Form C. 2121.

Prefix **SB** Code **HSA** m. Words **84** Charge APPENDIX 9 Recd. at **8.6A** m.
Office of Origin and Service Instructions **YIG**
Date **7/6/15**
From **Y/G**
By **Br Manft**

TO **CRA**

Sender's Number **1G13/5** Day of Month **16th** In reply to Number **AAA**

Indian Corps wire begins 1G 116 following from 1st Army no 1G 253 dated 15th begins following from 2nd Army begins General DU BOIS has conveyed information to 5th Corps that prisoners taken yesterday confirm previous intelligence received a week ago that General attack by enemy is intended on 15th or 16th AAA Officers state that appearance of strong patrols today about 5 pm on MENIN road afford further corroboration ends addressed CRA and DEHRA DUN Bde repeated BAREILLY Bde

From **Meerut Divn**
Place
Time

Priority

MESSAGES AND SIGNALS. No. of Message 6

Army Form C. 2121.

APPENDIX 99

Recd. at 12.5 p.m.
Date 15-2-15
From YIG
By B/Richmond

TO: CRA

Sender's Number: 61247
Day of Month: 15th
AAA

Indian Corps wires begins G533 15th please detail Genl SCOTT to attend conference at Indian Corps Hdqrs tomorrow twelve noon aaa commander aeronautics first wing wishes discuss question arty observation with arty cmdrs of the three corps ends for compliance

From: MEERUT DIVN
Time: 11.55 AM

LIST OF HOSTILE BATTERIES OPPOSITE M E E R U T
DIVISIONAL ARTILLERY, WITH THEIR TARGET NUMBERS
AND MAP POSITIONS :-

100 b

Target No.	Map Position	Remarks.
21	S 6 a 4 2	
23	S 6 d 7 8	
3b	S 17 b 4 5	
52	S 17 d 6 8	
52b	S 17 d 8 9	
46	S 18 a 5 3	
7a	S 21 d 2 1	
7	S 22 c	
25	S 23 a 4 9	
55a	S 23 d 10 9	
55b	S 23 c 8 8	
6a	S 28 b 9 10	
3a	S 29 b 9 4	
5	S 30 d 2 6	
34	T 14 c	
1b	T 19 c	
1c	T 19 c	
43	T 26 c 6 8	
4c	A 6 b 9 5	
4b	A 6 c 5 9	
41	A 12 d 9 4	
17	R 1 d 5 5	
56	B 7 a 4 5	
4d	S 29 d 6 3	

LIST OF OTHER OBJECTIVES :-

57	S 16 b	Plantation.
50	S 10 b 5 9	Pumping Station.
59	S 16 a 5 6	White House
61	S 17 a 7 4	Distillery.
60	S 17 c 10 6	House (R F H in V.)
53	S 21 c 4 5	Orchard.
54	S 22 a 5 5	School House
55	S 23 b 8 1	Red House
58	S 21 c 9 8	House (isolated)
S.H.	S 26 b 8 6	Snipers House
P.H.	S 23 b 7 3	Piquet House
G.S.	S 20 b 4 4	House with green shutter
H.R.	S 26 b 4 8	House on right of Shrine
K.1.	S 4 d	Cross roads S 4 d.
K.2.	S 17 a 7 8	Cross roads S 17 a.
K.3.	S 21 c 6 1	Cross roads S 21 c.
M.1.	S 20 b	Trench (S)
M.2.	S 26 c 10 6	do.
M.3.	S 27 b 2 9	do.

Major telephone connections of RA Meerut

SECRET

——— lets to be taken into Trenches or O.P.s

——— 8th Divl Sigs

Not to in —

R.O.C. Meerut Divn

Meerut Siege

C.R.A. 8th Divn

8" Siege

33rd Bde RFA (8th Divn)

H.Q. 2ff Bde

4in Rdr

13" Bde

110

113

114

OP Rue du Bois

2 Siege

9in Rdr

H.Q. 1ff Bde

36th Bde (2nd Divn)

OP Brewery

9.2"

OP Pont Fixe

C.R.A. 2nd Divn

MESSAGES, SIGNALS AND FIELD TELEGRAPHS

APPENDIX 102

Army Form C. 2121. Modified for India. No. of Message 15

Recd. at 8.45 P.m
Date 16/2/15
From 1 Corps
By M A Slatesp

TO CRA

NOTHING TO BE WRITTEN BY THE ADDRESSOR ABOVE THIS LINE.

Sender's Number.	Day of Month.	In reply to number.	AAA
G289 D/1	16th		

Wire from Indian Corps begins G58 16th aaa Fortyfourth Howitzer Bde consisting of 56th 47th and 60th Btys allotted to Indian Corps aaa Bde HQ and two last named Btys with due proportion Bde Amn Col joining from 1st Corps 19th Feb aaa Bde HQ and one Bty allotted to Meerut and one Bty to Lahore but Bde HQ will be attached temporarily to Lahore Divn now in front line aaa Wire 1st Corps direct where these units should be sent aaa Addressed Lahore & Meerut Divns ends aaa for early report

FROM Meerut Divn
Place
Time 7.30 PM

Army Form C. 2121. Modified for India. APPENDIX 108 No. of Message 2

Recd. at 9.15 a.m
Date F 1st 18/2/15
From Y 15
By G n Graysond

TO CRA

Sender's Number: G 289 D/3
Day of Month: 18

Now decided that 43rd How Bde will join Indian Corps aaa consists of thirtieth Bty now with first Corps and fortieth and fifty seventh Batteries now with fourth Corps aaa Thirtieth How Bty will join meerut Div today and has been directed to LECHEME representative to report to you at LILLERS aaa fifty sixth bty will be transferred to first corps aaa further instructions will follow as regards moves involved

FROM MEERUT DIVN
Time: 8.10 am

"A" Form.
Army Form C. 2121.

MESSAGES AND SIGNALS.

No. of Message _____

Prefix ____ Code ____ m. | Words. | Charge. | APPENDIX 10 | Recd. at ____ m.
Office of Origin and Service Instructions. | | This message is on a/c of: | | Date ____
Oxford | Sent At ____ m. | | Service. | From ____
 | To ____ | | (Signature of "Franking Officer.") | By ____
 | By ____ | | |

TO { MEERUT DIVISIONAL ARTILLERY

| Sender's Number | Day of Month | In reply to Number | AAA |
| G102 | 18th | BM 197 | |

30th How: Battery should relieve 56th How Battery at 3. a.m tomorrow and accompanied by Bde and Divl Ammn. Col Borhous should march GONNEHEM - HINGES - LOCON PONT TOURNANT LE TOURET and 40th How Bty is temporarily attached to MEERUT Division and should march to L'ECLEME tomorrow under arrangements between you and 8th Division. AAA Send officer 30th Battery to report LAHORE Divisional Artillery LOCON before arrival of battery.

From LAHORE Divisional Artillery
Place
Time

The above may be forwarded as now corrected. (Z)

Censor. | Signature of Addressor or person authorised to telegraph in his name

* This line should be erased if not required.

MESSAGES, SIGNALS AND FIELD TELEGRAPHS.

Army Form C. 2121. Modified for India.

APPENDIX 105

Recd. at 4.30 p.m
Date 18.2.15
From VIG
By G. Grayson

TO C.R.A Meerut

Sender's Number: G 289/6
Day of Month: 18th

AAA Indian Corps direct that 30th Battery be sent forward into front line (under LAHORE Division temporary) marching from L'ECLEME tomorrow AAA Fortieth Battery will join the LAHORE Division tomorrow and go into rest billets at L'ECLEME AAA please arrange accordingly addressed C.R.A Meerut repeated LAHORE Division for information

FROM Place: MEERUT Division
Time: 3.50 P.M

APPENDIX 106

Copy No. ...6....

OPERATION ORDER No.18.
by
Brigadier General A.B. SCOTT, C.B., D.S.O.,
Commanding MEERUT DIVISION.

BUSNES, 20 February 1915.

Reference Map:-
France - BETHUNE Sheet
1:40,000.

Intention. 1. The MEERUT Divn will relieve the LAHORE Divn in the front line on the 21st February 1915 and subsequent days.

Movements. 2. Moves of the Infantry Brigades and Divisional Troops will be as per march table attached.

Reliefs of units in trenches. 3. The reliefs of troops in the trenches will be carried out by the Brigadiers concerned, in direct communication with each other. Brigadiers of the LAHORE Divn will remain in command of their respective fronts until the reliefs of their troops have been completed when the relieving Brigadiers will assume command. Hours of assuming command will be at once reported to Divisional Headquarters.

Artillery. 4. The Artillery of the MEERUT Divn will relieve that of the LAHORE Divn on 25th and 26th February under the orders of the Divisional C.R.A.s.

Handing over of equipment. 5. The relieving Brigades will take over from those relieved the gum boots, braziers, periscopes, hand-grenades, trench guns, and mortar bombs, now in the trenches, which the G.O.C. LAHORE Divn has agreed to hand over.

Refilling. 6. Units will refill supplies at their new refilling points on the day of marching. Detailed instructions are being issued to all concerned.

Headquarters 7. The various Headquarters will open at LOCON as follows:-

    Divisional H.Q.   at 10.0 A.M. on 24th.
    Divisional Engineer H.Q.   at 10.0 A.M. on 24th.
    Divisional Artillery H.Q.   at noon on 26th.

Command. 8. The G.O.C. LAHORE Divn will remain in command of the front line and area until 10.0 A.M. on 24th., when the G.O.C. MEERUT Divn will assume command.

Lieut.-Col.
General Staff,
MEERUT DIVISION.

Issued at 9.0 A.M. by Signal Coy.
Copy No. 1 to Indian Corps,
    2   Lahore Divn
    3   Dehra Dun Bde
    4   Garhwal Bde
    5   Bareilly Bde
    6   C.R.A.
    7   C.R.E.
    8   4th Ind. Cavalry
    9   107th Ind. Pioneers
    10   Meerut Signal Coy
    11   A.Q.M.G.
    12   D.A.A.G.
    13   D.A.A. & Q.M.G.
    14   Divnl Train

Copy No. 15 C. of E. Chaplain
    16   A.D.M.S.
    17   2nd Divn
    18   8th Divn
    19
    20   War Diary
    21   & files
    22
    23

MARCH TABLE.

(Appendix to MEERUT Divn Operation Order No.18.)

Serial No.	Date.	Units.	From.	To.	Route.	Remarks.
1	2	3	4	5	6	7
1.	Feby. 21st	Garhwal Bde	LA COUTURE	Trenches (Southern Section)		Under orders to be issued by G.O.C. Lahore Divn.
2.	Feby. 22nd	Dehra Dun Bde	CALONNE & S.W. LA COUTURE	Le CORNET MALO(C.27.b)	Le CORNET MALO(C.27.b) – C.28.d – La Cix HARMUSE – R.21.b – ZELOBES.	To be clear of Le' CORNET MALO cross roads (C.28.d) by 10.0 A.M., including supply wagons which will follow Brigade.
3.	do.	No.2 Coy Train	CALONNE	Neighbour-hood of FOSSE(a)	do.	(a) Into billets to be indicated later.
4.	23rd	Dehra Dun Bde	LA COUTURE	Trenches (Northern Section.)		To be arranged by Lahore Divn
5.	do.	No.4 Coy S.& M.	CALONNE	LE TOURET	CALONNE, QUENTIN, PACAUT, PARADIS, R.25.c – C.36.b.99 – LES LOBES – ZELOBES –	To be clear of South end of CALONNE by 9.0 A.M.
6.	do.	No.130 I.F.A. No.20 B.F.A.	CALONNE ST FLORIS	LOCON	To follow No.4 Coy S.& M. to C.36.b.99 and thence via CORNET MALO to LOCON.	
7.	do.	107th Ind. Pion--eers.	L'ECLEME	Les FACONS	V.10.b – GONNEHEM – W.13.d – HINGES – AVELETTE – W.18.b – X.20.c – X.15.b –	Leaving billets not earlier than 10.30 A.M.
8.	24th	Bareilly Bde	CALONNE & N.W.	LA COUTURE	CALONNE, QUENTIN, PACAUT, PARADIS, C.24.d – R.21 – ZELOBES.	To be clear of south end of CALONNE by 9.0 a.m., in-cluding supply wagons which will follow brigade.
9	do.	No. 4 Coy Train	CALONNE	Neighbour-hood of FOSSE (b)	do. do.	(b) Into billets to be indicated later.

(contd)

March Table (contd).

1.	2	3	4	5	6	7
	Feby					
10.	24th	A.B./19 B.F.A. C.D./19 B.F.A.	CALONNE) RCBECQ)	VIELLE CHAPELLE	Unite at C.28.d at 10.30 A.M. and march via la Cix l'ARMUSE - R.21 - to ZELOBES.	
11.	do.	128 I.F.A.	BACQUEROLLES Fme	ZELOBES	To rendezvous with 19 B.F.A. at C.28.d and follow it as far as ZELOBES.	
12.	do.	Divnl H.Q.	BUSNES	LOCON	LILLERS & BETHUNE	
13.	do.	4th Ind Cavalry	HAMEL BILLET	La TOMBE WILLOT	BUSNES, GONNEHEM, Le VERTANNOY, HINGES, LOCON.	Leaving billets not earlier than 10.30 A.M.
14.	25th	Bareilly Bde	LA COUTURE	Trenches (Southern Section)		To be arranged later.
15.	do.	Garhwal Bde	Trenches (Southern Sect)	LA COUTURE		do. do.
16.	do.	No.3 Coy S.& M.	St FLORIS	RICHEBOURG	CALONNE, CUINCHY, PACAUT, PARADIS, C.24.d -R.21.b - ZELOBES.	Clearing South end of CALONNE by 9.0 A.M.

NOTE:- No. 3 Coy Meerut Divnl Train and No. 129 I.F.A. will stand fast in their present billets at L'EPINETTE and PARADIS respectively.

"A" Form. APPENDIX 107 Army Form C. 2121.
MESSAGES AND SIGNALS.

| Prefix | Code | m. | Words. | Charge. | This message is on a/c of: | Recd. at | m. |

TO { C.R.A.

| Sender's Number | Day of Month | In reply to Number | AAA |
| G.A 17/2 | 22nd | | |

Indian corps intimates that approval has been given to the following appointment:—

× × × × ×

Colonel (temporary Brigadier General) H. ST. C. LECKY (now Brigadier General R.A. attached Headquarters Indian Cavalry Corps) to command Royal Artillery Meerut Division vice Colonel (temporary Brigadier General) A. B. SCOTT C.B. D.S.O., and to retain his temporary rank

× × × × ×

Date Br. Genl. LECKY takes over his duties to be reported in due course.

From
Place Meerut Division
Time

MESSAGES AND SIGNALS.

APPENDIX 108

Recd. at 2.18 P m.
Date 23/2/15
From X/G
By Chapman

TO: CRA Meerut Div

Sender's Number: G290/21
Day of Month: 23rd

AAA

Indian Corps wires begins G679 reference opperations order no 55 5th Bde Field Arty will not be relieved for present addressed Lahore Div repeated Meerut Div ends wire which Bde remains in reserve

From Place: Meerut Div
Time: 1.30 Pm

APPENDIX 109
18

OPERATION ORDERS

by

Brigadier General R.St.C. LECKY, R.A. G.O.C., R.A. MEERUT DIVISION.

References:-
(Map – FRANCE BETHUNE) 1/40,000

LILLERS. 24th February '15.

INTENTION. 1. With reference to paragraph 4 of MEERUT Division Operation Order No.15 dated 24th February 1915 the MEERUT Divisional Artillery will relieve the LAHORE Divisional Artillery in the front line as follows:-
25th February – 4th Brigade R.F.A. will relieve 11th Bde R.F.A.
          (13th Brigade R.F.A. "   " 13th Bde R.F.A.
26th February (Meerut Divisional)   "   " (Lahore Divisional
          (Ammunition Column)   (Ammunition Column

MOVEMENTS. 2. Routes and times of starting are given in accompanying March Table. Special attention is invited to column "Remarks".

GROUPING. 3. (a) 4th Brigade R.F.A., 13th Brigade R.F.A. 18th Battery
North Section. (less 1 section)(temporarily) will be grouped with the DEHRA DUN Brigade in the NORTHERN Section of the line.
Artillery Group Commander:- Lt Colonel L.A.C. GORDON, R.F.A.

(b) 5th Brigade R.F.A.(of LAHORE Divisional Artillery) and
South Section. 30th Howitzer Battery R.F.A. will be grouped with the GARHWAL Brigade in the SOUTHERN Section of the line.
Artillery Group Commdr:- Lt Colonel L.G.F. GORDON, D.S.O., R.F.A.

Heavy Artillery. The 108th, 110th and 114th Heavy Batteries, and the 2nd and 8th Siege Batteries R.G.A. will come under the immediate command of the G.O.C., R.A., MEERUT Division, from the time he assumes command of the Artillery on the line.

TELEPHONIC 4. Under arrangement with the G.O.C., R.A. LAHORE Division the
COMMUNICATION whole of the existing telephone wire will be taken over as it stands by the relieving units, who will hand back to LAHORE Divisional Artillery the amounts they received from them at the last "relief".

SUPPLIES. 5. Units will refill with supplies in accordance with MEERUT Division memorandum No.Q.A/59 dated 23rd February 1915.

RAILHEAD. 6.   SUPPLIES ..... LILLERS.
         AMMUNITION... St VENANT.

COMMAND. 7. The G.O.C., R.A., LAHORE Division is remaining in command of the Artillery on the line until 12 noon on the 26th February 1915 at which time the G.O.C. R.A. MEERUT Division will assume command.

REPORTS 8. REPORTS to LOCON.

ROUTINE 9. Special attention is again invited to the orders on
STANDING equipment of stables, Artillery being left clean, "March
ORDERS. discipline", also to MEERUT Division General Staff Memorandum No.Gen.Sec/15 dated the 8th February 1915.
All Routes should be thoroughly reconnoitred beforehand.

                                          MAJOR R.A.
                           Brigade Major, Royal Artillery,
                             MEERUT DIVISION.

Issued at 7.o.p.m.
By Motor cyclist.

Copy No. 1 to General Staff MEERUT Divn. Copy No. 10 to O.C. 30th How. Battery.
" 2 to G.O.C., R.A. LAHORE Divn. " 11 to O.C. MEERUT Divl.
" 3 to G.O.C. BAREILLY Brigade.   Ammunition Column
" 4 to G.O.C. DEHRA DUN Brigade. " 12 to O.C.108th(H) Battery
" 5 to G.O.C. GARHWAL Brigade " 13 to O.C.110th(H) Battery
" 6 to O.C. 4th Brigade R.F.A. " 14 to O.C.114th(H) Battery
" 7 to O.C. 9th Brigade R.F.A. " 15 to O.C.2nd SIEGE Btty.
" 8 to O.C. 13th Brigade R.F.A. " 16 to O.C. 8th " "
" 9 to O.C. Headquarters R.F.A. " 17 to FILE.
                                           " 18 to WAR DIARY.

MARCH TABLE
MEERUT DIVISIONAL ARTILLERY.

Date.	Unit.	Starting point	Time.	Destination.	Route	Remarks.
25.2.15.	4th Bde R.F.A. (less Brigade Ammn Col)	Cross Roads P.29.b.8*3.	9.a.m.	LA CROIX BARBEE.	PONT LEVIS P.36.a.8*7, Mt BERNENCHON, LES HARISOIRS, LE CORNET MALO (Q.28), LA CIX NAR- MUSE, FOSSE, X roads R.29. b.d., - LA CROIX BARBEE.	Head of column not to arrive at Cross Roads in Q.24.d. before 10.30.am Resting battery marches in rear of other two batteries and proceeds in to billets in LA CIX MARMUSE.
25.2.15.	4th Bde R.F.A. Ammn Column.	CROSS ROADS P.29.b.8*3.	9.15 a.m.	ZELOBES	As above as far as X roads in Q.24.d.5*1 and then direct to ZELOBES.	Takes up supply of S.A.A to DEHRA DUN Brigade and 18.pr. Ammunit- ion to 4th Bde R.F.A. at 1.p.m
25.2.15.	9th Bde R.F.A. (less 1 battery and Bde Ammn Column.	CALONNE Bridge	9.a.m	LE TOURET	CALONNE Bridge, QUENTIN, PACAUT, cross roads Q.24.d, LES LOBES, ZELOBES, LA COUTURE - LE TOURET.	Rear of column to be clear of Cross roads at Q.24.d. by 10. a.m.
25.2.15.	9th Bde R.F.A. Ammun Column.	CALONNE Bridge.	9.5. a.m.	LE CASSAN.	Above route to LA COUTURE and then direct to LE CASSAN.	Takes up supply of S.A.A to BAREILLY Brigade and 18 pr. Ammuni- tion to 9th Bde R.F.A. at 1.p.m. Rear of column to be clear of cross roads at Q.24.d. by 10.30.a.m.
26.2.15.	13th Bde R.F.A. (less Brigade Ammn Column).	PONT LEVIS P.36.a.8*8.	7.45 a.m.	RICHEBOURG St VAAST.	Mt BERNENCHON, LES HARISOIRS, LE CORNET MALO (Q.28), LES LOBES, ZELOBES, LA COUTURE- RICHEBOURG St VAAST.	To clear LOCON- LESTREM road by 9.45.a.m. Resting battery disjoins at X roads Q.30.b. 5*10 and pro- ceeds into billets at LA CIX MARMUSE.
26.2.15.	13th Bde R.F.A. Ammun Column.	PONT LEVIS P.36.a.8*8.	8.15 a.m.	ZELOBES	As above as far as cross roads Q.30.b. 5*10 and then direct to position.	Takes up supply of 18 pr. ammunition to 13th Bde R.F.A. and S.A.A. to Infantry Bde in Divisional Reserve from 12.noon.
26.2.15.	MEERUT Divl Amn Column.	Cross roads P.19.a.	8 a.m.	PARADIS	BUSNES, ROBECQ, PONT LEVIS P.36.a.8*8, Mt BERNENCHON, LE CORNET MALO (Q.26)-PARADIS.	Takes up the supply of ammunition from 12 noon.

"A" Form. APPENDIX 110 Army Form C. 2121.
MESSAGES AND SIGNALS. No. of Message 15

Prefix SM Code DCP m. Words 34 Charge.
Office of Origin and Service Instructions: YIG

This message is on a/c of:

Recd. at 4.55 p.m.
Date 7IG 23/2/17
From YIG
By Br Stampa

TO { CRA Meerut through YIG

Sender's Number: G290/32
Day of Month: 25th
In reply to Number: 258 RA(4)
A A A

Suggested move of two batteries
9th Bde sanctioned aaa You
may carry out the move as soon
as you wish via CALONNE and
L'EPINETTE

From Meerut Divn

INTELLIGENCE SUMMARY UP TO 11.p.m.
5th February 1915.

1. The following hostile batteries were active to-day:-
   17, 5(from a position apparently in T 25 c)..

2. A battery was seen in S 5 d-exact location is required.

3. RICHEBOURG St VAAST was shelled by a battery reported as being in the direction of the BOIS du BIEZ.

4. There was considerably more germans in the trenches in S 21 a, S 20 b and d and S 26 b and d than usual. A few wore conspicuous red shoulder straps.

5. 8th Division report that the battery which shelled LA COUTURE yesterday was one near BAS POMMEREAU and that they are trying to knock it out.

6. A striped paper balloon was dropped about 9.a.m. from a german aeroplane to-day and fell near FOSSE. (see 10 below)

7. 56 has an alternative pair of emplacements at B 7 b 18. This was shelled to-day and a direct hit obtained. (Aeroplane observation).

8. 46 has emplacements just W. of the road at S 18 a 40. to S 22 b 05.

9. A track runs from S ∮ 23 c 05/ N. of this track at about S 22 b 53 there is a house in a green compound which seems to be used by the enemy.

10. One of our Morane-Saulnier monoplanes fought a german plane to-day and forced it to come down in the german lines after knocking several pieces off it.

N.W. Lynch-Staunton

Major R.A.,
Brigade Major, Royal Artillery,
MEERUT Division.

INTELLIGENCE SUMMARY UP TO 11 p.m. 6th FEBRUARY 1915.

1. Hostile Artillery shelled the following localities to-day:-
   (a) RUE du BOIS.
   (b) Trenches in S 20 and S 31 (field guns).
   (c) Neighbourhood of RUE de L'EPINETTE (15 cm. How:)
   (d) E. of RICHEBOURG St VAAST (light How: & field guns)
   In the case of (b) the battery was 6a.
   " (c) the battery was apparently 43 and the shells had practically no effect.
   " (d) The shells appeared to come from the direction of BAS POMMEREAU.
   " (a) the offending battery or batteries have been variously reported as being 5, 6a, 17, 56, 58 or 58b and as a howitzer and a gun.
   It seems unlikely that so much hostile artillery fire should be concentrated on the RUE du BOIS.

2. The shelling of the trenches by 6a was apparently a reply to a combined shoot at enemy's works in S 20 b by 2nd Siege Battery and 44th Battery R.F.A.

3. The operation carried out between CUINCHY and the railway triangle by the Guards Brigade this afternoon was completely successful.

4. One of the 6" guns of the 8th Siege Battery to-day achieved a record by getting off 21 rounds in 15 minutes.

5. An air report from 2nd Division states that there are new gun emplacements at A 23 a 7 7 just in the V formed by the dotted roads.

6. 2nd Siege Battery reported more Germans than usual in early morning in Redoubt S 26 b 3 2, also at Lone Tree trench S 21 a 9.

Major R.A.,

Brigade Major, Royal Artillery,
MEERUT DIVISION.

INTELLIGENCE SUMMARY UP TO 10.30.p.m. 7th FEBRUARY 1915.

I. Hostile Artillery shelled the following localities to-day:-

    1. Position of 71st Battery at LOISNE.
    2. RUE du BOIS.
    3. Road Junction at S 15 a 1'8 (one round daily)
    4. 7th Battery observation post (at 4.p.m.), at the
    5. "Ritz" presumably by 52(or 5).
    5. Old position of "N" Battery R.H.A. S. of Cse de RAUX.
Insufficient data for location of these batteries received.

II. (a) Scouts from 58th Rifles report what looked like 2 guns at 7a(S.21.d. 2'1.)
    (b) An airmen spotted a flash at S 5 d 9'9 a few days ago. Possibly the battery it is desired to locate in that vicinity? Further confirmation desirable.
    (c) Another Airman feels confident 5 is active from Orchard at S 30 b 3'0. This is corroborated by a shell scoop of a 15 c.m. shell which fell near 20th Battery at 4.p.m.

III. 1. More activity reported in trenches at S 21 a 9'8.
    2. 14th Battery shelled machine gun in enemy trench at S 10 b with good effect. Infantry Commander reported screams from the trench !
    3. Enemy in big Redoubt in front of PIQUET HOUSE are wearing grey Brodrick caps with a broad red band.
    4. Searchlight located at S 15 d 2'8 by cross bearings at 8.30.p.m. on 8th February by 44th Battery and shelled.

IV. INDIAN CORPS states:-
    (a) At about 7.a.m. a party of Germans approached 3rd Coldstreams shouting "don't shoot, we are engineers" about 30 killed, machine gun assisting.
    (b) About 4.p.m. enemy shelled trenches and PONT FIXE road very heavily.
    At 5.p.m. shelling slackened and an attempt to advance by enemy was stopped by our Artillery.

Major R.A.,

Brigade Major, Royal Artillery,
MEERUT DIVISION.

INTELLIGENCE SUMMARY UP TO 10.p.m. 8th FEBRUARY 1915.

I. Hostile Artillery shelled the following localities to-day:
   (a) RUE du BOIS - variously reported as being 52 (or 5 possibly) 1b or 6a ?.
   (b) 7th Battery Observation post.

II. <u>Air Reconnaissance</u>
An early morning reconnaissance carried out by Lieut POWELL gave the following emplacements as occupied to-day:-
  1. 6a...S 28 b 9'8.
  2. 6a...S 29 a 8'9 - emplacements round haystacks.
  3. 5....S 30 d 2'9 - (in orchard).
  4.46....S 18 a 5'0
The following were definitely empty:-
  1.   S 12 a 3'0.
  2.   T 1 c 3'5.
  3.   N 31 c 8'2.
  4.   S 6 b 5'5.
The following were doubtful:-
  1.21....S 6 a 5'5.
  2.   S 5 d 9'9 - Position on West of BOIS du BIEZ between it and farm, shadows made observation of this very difficult.

A later air report received at 1.15.p.m. gave 4 emplacements at A 6 a 5'1 (4b) as occupied.

III. During the day odd rounds were fired at the DISTILLERY (S 17 a 7'4), VIOLAINES Distillery, LA BASSEE Observation Station and the White House (S 16 a 5'0), by our Heavy Batteries - this seemed to have the effect of checking hostile Artillery fire.

IV. 114th Heavy Battery working with Airman engaged 5, (S 30 d 2'9) and found the range.
Same battery also engaged 6a (S 29 a 8'9) and put 4 rounds into this battery.
Same battery obtained 3 hits on house at S 22 b 5'3 out of 11 shots, with airman also.

V. At 4.30.p.m. a combined bombardment of 4b (A 6 a 5'1) by 110th and 114th Heavy Batteries and 8th Siege Battery (6" gun) took place, result not yet known.

VI. More work reported proceeding in LONE TREE TRENCH (S 21 a 9'6).
Germans have been noticed wearing caps similar to our troops soft winter cap.
About 12 noon, a railway engine was seen pushing trucks in Northerly direction behind ILLIES from neighbourhood of R in RICHEBOURG L'AVOUE.

                                                R.M. Lynch-Staunton.

                                                Major R.A.,

Brigade Major, Royal Artillery,
      MEERUT DIVISION.

INTELLIGENCE SUMMARY UP TO 10.P.M. 8th FEBRUARY 1915.

I. Hostile batteries shelled the following places to-day:-
(a) RUE du BOIS (i) Field Guns probably 5- fragment of lining found.
(ii) Light Howitzers (105 mm)- base plug found,- probably 5a.b.
(iii) Either 105 mm Howitzer or 110 mm gun from direction of LORGIES (fragment of base of shell found).
(b) Neighbourhood of RICHEBOURG St VAAST.
(c) Trenches N.W. of GIVENCHY.
(d) Ground immediately N.W. of Cse du RAUX with black powder shell- fuze commonly found with 15 cm. Howitzer found
(e) Trenches E. of Brewery with H.E.

II. The only hostile battery actually seen to be active was 4b A 6 b 5'1.
Shells which have fallen in 2nd Battery billet appear to come from 4c A 5 b 2'5 and 5R S 17 d 6'6.
The fuze of a shell which burst yesterday at F 4 c 10'6 was a very light aluminium one set at extreme graduation

III. The following localities were engaged to-day with a few rounds:-
3c, 51, 4b, 6a, 54, 80,
VIOLAINES O.P.
S 15 d 2'0- apparently a new M.G. emplacement.
RUE d'OUVERT and neighbourhood of P.E.
M.G. in S 10 b.
4 men out of 6 knocked over crossing barricade in S 5 c,
BOIS du BIEZ.
House S 11 a 9'4.
House S 11 b 11 a probable observation Post- (excellent effect obtained with H.E.)
House S 5 d 5'6
Enemy sniping O.P. from trenches.
M.G. in enemy trench S 9 d.
Working party in S 21 and 22 engaged at mid-night 8th/9th by arrangement with infantry.

Also Red roofed house in A 10 a, close to GIVENCHY-LORGIES ridge- a probable observation post for fire towards GIVENCHY.

IV. The enemy are using their waterproof sheets as lean-to protections in rear of head cover.
They also relieve nature flagrantly in the open and wrap paper round their legs before readjusting their trousers.
Steady work continued on LONE TREE Trench and Redoubt behind Shrine S 21 a 2'6 and S 22 b and d.

CORRECTION:- Reference Summary dated 8th February 1915-
II. 2. Emplacements of 2½ round haystacks should have been described as S 22 a 2'5 and not as therein stated.

Major R.A.
Brigade Major, Royal Artillery,
MEERUT DIVISION.

INTELLIGENCE SUMMARY UP TO 11.30.p.m. 10th February 1915.

I. The following localities were shelled by hostile artillery
to-day:-
 (a) O.P. in RUE du BOIS by No.5(field guns).
 (b) Vicinity of RUE du BOIS(s.14) by 15 cm. howitzers
     apparently from E. of BOIS du BIEZ(probably 21 or 23)
 (c) PORT ARTHUR S. 4. d. by field guns near eb.
 (d) BOIS du BOIS S b by light howitzers.

II. The following were shelled to-day with air observation:-
    a4 PLOUICH(registered only for combined operations
       with 8th Division).
    a5 No effect, signalling lamp broke down.
    B4 something blown up.

 Following by visual observation or previous registry:-

    A was bombarded by 110th and 114th Heavy Batteries
       at 4.15.p.m.
    P.H.
    Redoubt just N.W. of 63.
    New M.G. emplacement in S.15.
    Barricade at S 10 b a'8- good effect obtained by
    2nd Siege Battery, parapet completely breached.
    Redoubt S 10 b, Shrine Redoubt, Western Redoubt
    A R b 2'5.
    The following places were registered:-
       Trenches in S 15 d 2'6.
       "   " S 10 b 3'8.
       51
       VIOLAINES Distillery.

III. A communicating trench has been made in front of Redoubt
     W. of P.H. to sandbag Redoubt about 50 yards N.W.
     Men wearing shakos were seen in the Redoubt N.W. of 63.
     The trenches seem to be very lightly held, the parapets
     are mostly sandbag ones and several houses in rear of
     the german line are loopholed and have had apertures
     constructed which would easily accommodate M.G's.
     A certain amount of work was going on in a Redoubt just
     W of road about S 10 b n'8.
     A sap commenced from W. corner of salient in S. 21 a.
     Some work has been carried out in Shrine Redoubt.

                                    Major R.A.

                          Brigade Major, Royal Artillery.
                                 MEERUT DIVISION.

INFORMATION SUMMARY UP TO 11.30.p.m. 11th FEBRUARY 1915.

1. The following localities were shelled during the day by Enemy Artillery:-
   (a) "RITZ" Factory by 5.9" from E. side of BOIS du BIEZ at 11.30.a.m.
   (b) "RITZ" at 12.15.p.m. variously reported as fired upon by:-
       (i) H.V. gun in direction of BEAU PUITS.
       (ii) 5.
       (iii) 5a.
       (iv) 5ab.
       This shelling ceased when DISTILLERY(51), and 5 and 5a were all simultaneously shelled by us in reply!
   (c) 7th Battery's Observation Post near "PORT ARTHUR" by field battery not located.
   (d) 20th Battery's old position in RUE des CHEVATTES at 11.a.m. with 5 rounds 15 cm. howitzers.
   (e) Observing station in RUE du BOIS at 3.40.p.m.- No.5 again suspected and shelled by us.

II. The following were shelled to-day by us:-
   1. With aerial observation by 110th Heavy Battery:- Position at S.5.d.5'5(S.W. corner BOIS du BIEZ) suspected on being a gun position. Effect reported as being all round target, and one round caused a considerable explosion.(much greater than a shell burst).
   2. With visual observation or by previous registry:-
      Batteries at- 5)suspected of shelling O.P. at
)12 noon. These by 110th and 114th
                    6a)Heavy Batteries simultaneously.

                    5 again at 3.40.p.m. by 110th Heavy Battery.
                    4c-by 114th Heavy Battery.
      10.30.a.m. Redoubt in S.10.b. near Pumping Station by 2nd Siege Battery in conjunction with 14th Battery R.F.A.- one good breech made.
      11.a.m..... House in S.11.c.4'2.
                    44th Battery fired at Salient in S.20. A H.E. shell smashed in the end of a splinter proof and caused Germans to retire from there.
      12.15.p.m. Redoubt in S.10.d.2'2 by 2nd Siege and 2nd Battery R.F.A.-reported very effective.
      2.30.p.m. Same Redoubt again, several Germans having returned in the interval to repair it- good effect.
      12.25.p.m. DISTILLERY(51) shelled by 56th Howitzer Battery in conjunction with 44th Bty R.F.A.
      12.30.p.m. 44th Battery shelled splinter proof in front line trenches at S.15.d.3'7 using H.E. shell with good effect, also in conjunction with 56th Howitzer Battery.
      2.0.p.m. A few rounds at trench S.15.c.8'2 by 20th Battery.R.F.A.
      2.45.p.m. Machine Gun emplacement S.15.a.2'3 by 20th Battery R.F.A.
      3.38.p.m. Salient in S.20.b.10'4 by 2nd Siege Battery-last round very effective.

III. At 3.p.m. 14th Battery observed flashes at S.5.d.-doubtless battery at S.5.d.5'5. engaged by 110th Heavy Battery with airman during the day morning(This will be known in future as No.20.)
Enemy has improved and lengthened the wall of sandbags which is N.W. of PIQUET House Redoubt.
Enemy appeared very quiet in front of Southern Section of our line all day.

III continued.

Our Infantry report having seen many wounded passing along trench after yesterday's bombardment of barricade at S.10.b.2'2. Air reconnaissance this morning reports two elaborate new trenches being constructed. They run parallel to each other starting from a point in ESTAIRES-LA BASSEE Road East of G of RICHEBOURG L'AVOUE, running South of West for 100 yards and then N.W.

Major R.A.,
Brigade Major, Royal Artillery,
MEERUT DIVISION.

INTELLIGENCE SUMMARY UP TO 11.p.m. 12th FEBRUARY 1915.

I. The following localities were shelled by hostile batteries during the day:-
   (a) 2nd Battery observing station at "RITZ"- shelled at 9.45.a.m. and again at 11.5.a.m. Shelling ceased when this battery retaliated on enemy trenches in front of O.P.- Culprit reported as being No.5.
   (b) ESTAIRES-LA BASSEE road at 12.40.p.m.- by a battery of light field howitzers in neighbourhood of 8b (or close to the cross roads).
   (c) RUE du BOIS at 2.p.m. by hostile guns in neighbourhood of 52.

II. The following objectives were shelled to-day by us, by visual observation or previous registration:-
   (a) G U N S
      Hostile battery at 46) by 110th Heavy Battery at
      "   "   " 8b) 1.p.m.
      "   "   " 5 by 110th Heavy Battery at 2.20.p.m.
      "   "   " 5 by 110th Heavy Battery at 5.p.m.
      "   "   " 5 by 2nd Siege Battery at 10.35.a.m.
      "   "   " 5 by 114th Heavy Battery at 2.5.p.m.
      "   "   " 6a by 114th Heavy Battery at 2.5.p.m.

   (b) W O R K S
      Salient in S.20 by 44th Battery at 10.a.m.-effect with H.E. reported good on splinter proof.
      Redoubt at S.10d 3'8 by 2nd Siege and 7th Field Battery at 10.10.a.m. Effect reported excellent. 20 Germans bolted once.
      New German work at S.15.c. by 20th Battery at 12.45.p.m.
      At 2.p.m. a combined bombardment of Redoubt in S.10.d. by 4 Field Batteries of Northern Group, in which 56th Howitzer and 2nd Siege Batteries joined. the 110th and 114th Heavy Batteries by previous arrangement kept up a slow fire on enemy's Observation Posts during the operation, and prepared to neutralize any hostile battery which attempted to retaliate.
      This was the case with battery at S.30.d.8'9 which was immediately engaged. The operation is reported as having been most effective.
      LONE TREE TRENCH by 2nd Siege Battery at 1.25.p.m.
      Trench junction in S.11.c.5'6 by 2nd Siege Battery at 2.20.p.m.
      Shrine Redoubt by 2nd Siege Battery at 3.50.p.m. with very good effect.
      Trench in S.15.c.9'7 used as a living trench, by 20th Battery at 4.30.p.m.
   (c) PROBABLE OBSERVATION STATIONS.
      DISTILLERY S.17.a.7'4.   () House in S.11.d.1'4.
      VIOLAINES Distillery.   () House at S.11.c.4'4.
      White House S.16.a.5.0.   () House at S.24.b.8'2.

III. INFORMATION.
   About the usual number of Germans were noticed in the Redoubts and trenches.
   New White Cross in ORCHARD. No Shakos or Khaki Coats noticed to-day.
   There is a house at S.24.b.8'2 probably used as an Observation Post.
   Observation post of 110th Heavy Battery shelled 4 times during the day.

R.K. Lynch-Staunton.
Major. R.A.
Brigade Major, Royal Artillery.
MEERUT DIVISION.

INTELLIGENCE SUMMARY UP TO 11 p.m. 13th FEBRUARY 1915.

I. The following hostile batteries were active during the day:-
1. 5 which shelled the "RITZ" at 1.30.p.m.(also reported as battery at S.17.d.8'3).
2. A new battery at S.24.d.2'8 flashes of which were located at 2.25.p.m. while 5 was again shelling the "RITZ". It was engaged by 110th Heavy Battery apparently with good effect, showers of sparks being sent up twice.
3. 6a which was active about 2.p.m. but was silenced by our heavy howitzers.

II. Following objectives shelled by our Artillery during the day:-
(a) G U N S.
5)
6a) By heavy batteries.
53--by Field Battery.
S.24.d.2'8)
4c) By Heavy Batteries.

(b) L O C A L I T I E S.
Le PLOUICH)
BAS POMMERAU) From 10 to 10.15.a.m.by all our heavy
Batteries(except Siege) in co-operation with short bombardment of these localities by 7th and 8th Divisional Artillery.

(c) W O R K S.
Salient in S.20 and a new sandbag shelter 125 yards S. of the Salient. A few Germans left this shelter after it was hit.
M.G. emplacement in S.15.d.2'6.
Redoubt in S.15.a.
LONE TREE TRENCH, S.21.a.9'6, with excellent effect- after 3 rounds timber blown up in considerable quantities.
The Barricade(S.10.b.8'8) causing several casualties men seen carried away on stretchers.
A brushwood screen at cross roads at S.17.a.5'9 which concealed enemy's movements on LA BASSEE road.
Trench at S.21.a.1'8 reported to be newly occupied.
New earthworks under construction at S.20.d.8'8.

(d) OBSERVING STATIONS.
LORGIES   House at S.24.b.8'2.
VIOLAINES
DISTILLERY S.17.a.7'4.

III. INFORMATION.
Everything seemed very quiet all day along the front, with the exception of intermittant shelling of the "RITZ". Possibly one of our machine guns in outbuilding there is drawing this fire.
A few shell fell into RICHEBOURG between 2.30. and 3.p.m.
A small flag flying in trench about 500 yards S.E. of "RITZ":-

| BLUE |
| WHITE |
| RED |

During the day the 11th and 5th Brigades R.F.A. of the LAHORE Divisional Artillery relieved the 4th and 9th Brigades of the MEERUT Divisional Artillery.

MAJOR.R.A.
Brigade MAJOR, Royal Artillery,
MEERUT DIVISION.

INTELLIGENCE SUMMARY UP TO NOON 21st FEBRUARY 1915.

I. **HOSTILE ARTILLERY.**
Hostile artillery unusually active during the day.
Following batteries were firing:-

a)
b) (position not exactly located).
c)
d)
A Howitzer battery judged to be in T 13 d, but no flashes located.
A field battery in BOIS du BIEZ.
A field gun in still unknown exactly located.
A German "6in" Howitzer Battery of at least 4 guns, which shelled the 54th Battery from 4.50 p.m. to 5.15 p.m. This was immediately preceded by 4 rounds from the PIPSQUEAK battery firing from same locality. Most of the shell were blind, and were generally fired 4 at a time. Shell bursting in air reported as being heavier than those bursting on graze.
1) and 2) were also suspected to-day, but no confirmation received.

II. **OBJECTIVES ENGAGED.**
A battery in T 13 d, believed to be the one that shells RICHEBOURG St VAAST, by 110th Heavy Battery with aeroplane.
4d by same battery also with aeroplane.
2a by 2nd Siege Battery with aeroplane.
2) by 2nd Siege Battery with aeroplanes.
AUCHY, LA BASSEE & lives, Station and AUGERS were registered by 6th Siege Battery with aeroplane observation.
Registration continued by 7th and 8th Brigades R.F.A.

III. **INFORMATION.**
The RIFLES was active several times during the day. Machine guns behind TRIPE House both were firing a good deal morning and evening.
During the morning the 10th Brigade R.F.A. relieved the 15th Brigade R.F.A. with the Divisional Ammunition Column over the LAHORE Divisional Ammunition Column.

Major R.A.
Brigade Major, Royal Artillery,
MEERUT DIVISION.

INTELLIGENCE SUMMARY UP TO 11 P.M. 8TH FEBRUARY 1915.

I. HOSTILE ACTIVITY.

(a) RITZ – BUT du BOIS – RICHEBOURG st VAAST shelled at 10.a.m. by a heavy howitzer battery reported as being at S 30 c 3'4. This battery, flashes of which were seen by 110th Heavy Battery's observing officer, opened fire 4 times during the day. Fuze marked
K Z 14
J 14
(b) 48 opened fire twice, but stopped at once when shelled by 110th Heavy Battery.
(c) A battery in T 18 d shelled RICHEBOURG st VAAST during afternoon.
(d) Either 17 or else one of the VIOLAINES batteries appeared active at intervals.
(e) 2 H.V. field guns (PIPSQUEAK) located by flashes in S 36 c 3'4.
(f) FESTUBERT by a field howitzer battery.
(g) A 4'2 howitzer shelled old position of 24th Battery – shell appeared of latter quality

II. OBJECTIVES ENGAGED.

1. Heavy howitzer battery in S 30 c 3'4, by 110th and 108th Heavy Batteries, former observing for latter.
2. 4 b by 108th Heavy Battery.
3. 48 by 110th Heavy Battery.
4. 2 H.V. guns at S 36 b 3'4 by 2nd Siege Battery.
5. Salient in orchard by 2nd Siege Battery, some of the parapet was breached and some chevaux de frize and wire entanglement destroyed.
6. DISTILLERY, ORPAN HOUSE, LORGIES, WHITE HOUSE, houses in RUE du MARAIS and QUINQUE RUE suspected of being probable observing stations.

Major R.A.,
Brigade Major, Royal Artillery,
MEERUT DIVISION.

INTELLIGENCE SUMMARY UP TO 11 p.m. 26th FEBRUARY 1915.

I. HOSTILE ACTIVITY.

48. 48 opened fire during morning and afternoon, but ceased at once when fired at by 110th Heavy Battery.

4a A heavy howitzer at T.10.a.1.3, this is old position of 48, and will be known as such.
Battery at S.28.b.4.4 opened fire at 4.15.p.m.- was engaged by 35th Heavy Battery (2nd Division), observation by 8th Siege Battery's observing officer, who could distinguish the gun detachments working. Good effect obtained and battery silenced. PIPSQUEAK shelled RUE du BOIS O.P. at 8.30.a.m. and 1.p.m., also the Haystack O.P.- "crater" giving direction of SCHOOL HOUSE.

II. OBJECTIVES ENGAGED.

48 48 by 110th Heavy Battery (see above).
Battery at S.28.b.4.4 by 35th Heavy Battery (see above). Same battery at 5.45.p.m. by 8th Siege Battery with aeroplane (wireless observation).

4a Battery at T.10.a.1.3 (or 0.3) by 8th Siege Battery through 110th Heavy Battery's Observing officer.

8b 8b by 8th Siege Battery with aeroplane (wireless).
Barricade in S.6.c.4.4 by 14th Battery with same effect.
Working party behind fire trench in S.6.c. where considerable activity had been going on the last few days- by 14th Battery.-
Possible O.P.- house in S.6.d.8.7.

III. INFORMATION.

Very little movement noticed in German lines noticed today.
Only few men in salient near ORCHARD. Chevaux-de-Frise had been replaced here.
Usual number of men in LONE TREE Trench.
A certain amount of activity in trenches at S.10.c.- carrying planks etc.
About 7.30.a.m. several Periscopes seen in Redoubt in S.10.d, also much movement there. At 4.45.p.m. this Redoubt was seen to be on fire, high flames and dense smoke proceeding from it. A few more shell were then put into it.
No hostile aircraft seen to-day.

Major R.A.,
Brigade Major, Royal Artillery,
MEERUT DIVISION.

1:40,000

FRANCE (BETHUNE)

Handwritten notes (top):
Map showing position of R.A.
MEERUT Div. Feb 1915 and
location of targets.

To illustrate War diary
for Feb 1915
up to 14.2.15

R.A. burst: Black
numbers refer to blg. + columns

German guns etc: Blue
numbers refer to list of
targets issued to all units vide
appdx. 100b.

36ᵃ S.E. | 6 S.W.

36ᵃ N.E. | 36ᵃ N.W.

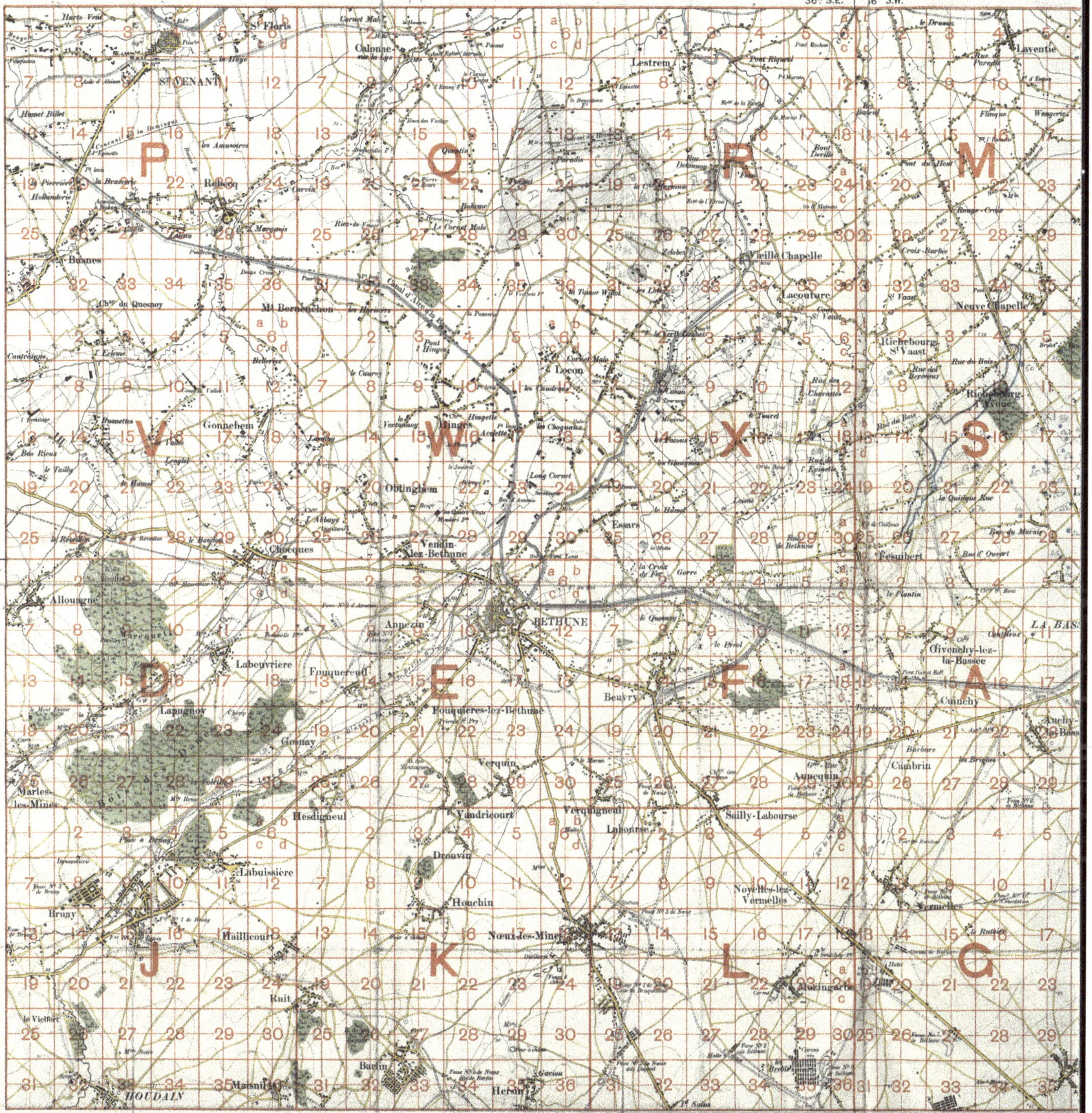

Geographical Section, General Staff, No. 2742.

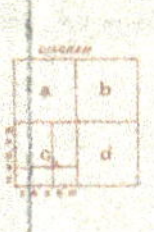

INSTRUCTIONS AS TO THE USE OF THE SQUARES.

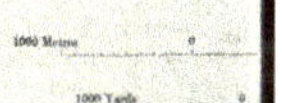

Meerut Division

1st To 31st January 1915

C. R. A.

WAR DIARY

of

C. R. A. Meerut Division.

1st January 1915 To 31st January 1915

WAR DIARY VOL VI

INTELLIGENCE SUMMARY.

(Erase heading not required.)

Army Form C. 2118.

Hour, Date, Place	Summary of Events and Information	Remarks and references to Appendices
1st January 1915. 11AM.	MEERUT Division resting. — Major R.K. LYNCH-STAUNTON, R.A., Brigade Major R.A. MEERUT Division proceeded to ENGLAND on 7 days Upon Vacation day.	MM2.2
2nd January 1915. 11AM.	Capt P.G. ROBINSON R.A. joined as Staff Captain R.A. MEERUT Division vice Major E.G. THOMPSON, 17th Lancers who rejoined unit.	MM2.2
3rd January 1915. 11AM.	MEERUT Division resting. the hand charges of Major R.K. LYNCH-STAUNTON RA Capt Indian Army No: 6779 on account of an accident which it met with whilst at exercise. (Capt D MACDONALD AVC)	MM2.2 / MM2.2
4th January 1915. 11AM.	do	MM2.2
5th January 1915. 11AM.	do	MM2.2
6th January 1915. 11AM.	MEERUT Division resting. During this day the Indian Corps Commander (Lieut General Sir J. WILLCOCKS K.C.B, K.C.S.I, K.C.M.G, D.S.O.) inspected the personnel of the R.A. units of the MEERUT Division	MM2.2
7th January 1915. 11AM.	MEERUT Division resting. Major R.K. LYNCH-STAUNTON, R.A., Brigade Major R.A. Meerut Division returned from leave.	MM2.2
8th January 1915. 11AM.	MEERUT Division resting. Brigadier General A.B. SCOTT, C.B, D S O G.O.C., R.A. MEERUT Division and his Orderly Officer and A.D.C. (Lieut J.N. MASON MACFARLANE, R.A.) proceeded on leave to ENGLAND for 7 days	MM2.2
9th January 1915. 11AM.	MEERUT Division resting	MM2.2
10th January 1915. 11AM.	do	MM2.2

Army Form C. 2118.

WAR DIARY (continued) VOL VI
INTELLIGENCE SUMMARY.
(Erase heading not required.)

Instructions regarding War Diaries and Intelligence Summaries are contained in F.S. Regs., Part II. and the Staff Manual respectively. Title pages will be prepared in manuscript.

Hour, Date, Place	Summary of Events and Information	Remarks and references to Appendices
11th January 1915. 11 A.M.	MEERUT Division resting	M29
12th do.	do.	M29.
13th do.	do	M29
14th do.	do	M29
15th do.	do	M29
16th do.	do	M29
17th do.	do.	M29.
18th do.	MEERUT Division resting. Captain P.G. ROBINSON, R.A. Staff Captain R.A., MEERUT Division proceeding to ENGLAND on 14 days leave.	M29. M29.
19th do.	MEERUT Division resting	M29.
20th do.	do	M29
21st do.	do	M29
22nd do.	do	M29
23rd do.	do.	M29.
24th do.	Proceeded into action to relieve 2 Brigade of the LAHORE Division who were with the Ind Corps. Brig General A.B.SCOTT, C.B., D.S.O. under orders from the MEERUT Divino proceeded to command of the two former Brigades and established his Headquarters at LES LOBES recordingly. Lt Colonel A.C. GORDON R.F.A. assumed duties of C.R.A. at 8.30 AM	M29.

Army Form C. 2118.

WAR DIARY (continued) VOL VI
or
INTELLIGENCE SUMMARY.
(Erase heading not required.)

Instructions regarding War Diaries and Intelligence Summaries are contained in F.S. Regs., Part II. and the Staff Manual respectively. Title pages will be prepared in manuscript.

Hour, Date, Place	Summary of Events and Information	Remarks and references to Appendices
25th January 1915. HAM.	MEERUT Division resting. During the day movements to new billeting areas was carried out in accordance with MEERUT Division No. G.220/1 dated 22.1.1915 and G.220/2 dated 23.1.1915; also MEERUT Divisional Artillery No. 169 R.A.(L) dated 24.1.15. An alteration was made in the march route of the MEERUT Divisional Ammunition Column vide C.R.A's R.A.S. 24 dated 25.1.15 and MEERUT Division No. G.220/3 dated 25.1.15; see also Brigade Major, R.A. MEERUT Division No. R.A.S. 25 dated 25.1.15.	x Appendix 73 x Appendix 74 & Appendix 75 × Appendix 76 * Appendix 77 & Appendix 78 MP29 MP29 MP23
12.45 p.m. do	Meerut Division intimate that 110th Heavy Battery to remain in constant state of readiness for next few days	⊕ Appendix 79 MP29 ⊘ Appendix 80
3.20 p.m. do	Meerut Division's 1122 received for 110th Heavy Battery to be sent to 2nd Division as soon as possible.	@ Appendix 81
3.55 p.m. do	Meerut Division's 1123 received giving march route of 110th Heavy Battery via LILLERS & BETHUNE to LOCON	
26th January 1915. HAM	MEERUT Division resting.	
1.13 p.m. do	8 Orders received for 56th How. Battery R.F.A. and Section of 44th Bde Amm Col to march soon as possible to CALONNE, to be attached to 4th Corps.	8 Appendix 82
5.30 p.m. do	Orders received that MEERUT Division be prepared to move at shortest notice in view of probable presence of great german troops in front of British positions.	oxo Appendix 83 MP29

WAR DIARY
or
INTELLIGENCE SUMMARY.
(Erase heading not required.)

Army Form C. 2118.

Instructions regarding War Diaries and Intelligence Summaries are contained in F.S. Regs., Part II. and the Staff Manual respectively. Title pages will be prepared in manuscript.

Hour, Date, Place	Summary of Events and Information	Remarks and references to Appendices
27th January 1915. 11 A.M.	MEERUT Division resting	
9.10 a.m.	*Orders received to maintain units in a condition of being able to turn out at two hours notice.	*appendix. 84
1.50 p.m.	*Orders received that only LAHORE Division will be kept in state of readiness	*appendix. 85. MOR 22
28th January 1915. 11 A.M.	MEERUT Division resting	MOR 33 MOR 9
29th January 1915. 11 A.M.	do.	
30th January 1915. 11 A.M.	do.	MOR 8
31st January 1915. 11 A.M.	R.F.A. acting C.R.A. MEERUT Division. During the day Lt Colonel. L.A.C. GORDON Brigade Major R.A. MEERUT Division and Major R.K. LYNCH-STAUNTON, R.A. R.A. MEERUT Division proceeded to LOCON to interview the R.A. Staff of the 2nd Divisional Artillery with regard to the MEERUT Divisional Artillery relieving the 2nd Divisional Artillery early next month. MEERUT Division noted. Intimation received regarding the redistribution of heavy and Howitzer batteries consequent on the MEERUT Divisional Artillery relieving the 2nd Divisional Artillery, the orders on this subject will be attached to next months volume of this diary as an appendix.	

M. Lynch-Staunton
Major R.A.
for C.R.A. Meerut Division

1st February 1915.

APPENDIX 73

No G. 220/1
Headquarters, Meerut Divn.
22nd January 1915.

Memorandum

The billeting areas of Brigades & Divisional Troops are reallotted as follows:-

(i) Dehra Dun Bde Area:-
  Attd troops:- 9th Bde R.F.A.
  No 4 Coy, S. & M.
  $\frac{A \& B}{19}$ B. F. A.
  No 128 S. F. A.

  Boundaries:-
  Point ¼ mile S.W. of + roads at BURBURE — FOSSE FERFAY No 3 (inclusive) — BELLERY (exclusive) — BAILLEUL les PERNES — AUMERVAL — FLORINGHEM (all inclusive) — FOSSE FERFAY No 1 (exclusive) — point ¼ mile S.W. of + roads at BURBURE.

(ii) Garhwal Brigade Area:-
  Attd troops:- 13th Bde R.F.A.
  No 3 Coy S. & M.
  $\frac{C \& D}{19}$ B. F. A.
  129 S. F. A.

  Boundaries:-
  LILLERS — LESDESSES (both exclusive) — LIERES — AMES (both inclusive) — FOSSE FERFAY No 3 (exclusive) — point ¼ mile S.W. of + roads at BURBURE — LILLERS (both exclusive).

(iii) Bareilly Brigade Area:-
  Attd troops:- 4th Bde R.F.A.
  $\frac{C \& D}{20}$ B. F. A.
  130 S. F. A.
  107th Pioneers

  Boundaries:-
  LILLERS — BOURECQ (both exclusive) — HAM (inclusive) — GUARBECQUE (exclusive) — LA PIERRIERE — LA MIQUELLERIE (both inclusive) — LILLERS (exclusive).

(iv) Divisional Troops Areas:-
  (a) Divisional Train — BOURECQ.
    56th (How) Battery R.F.A. } LESPESSES.
    110th (Heavy) Battery R.G.A. }
  (b) Meerut Divnl Ammn. Column — FONTAINE-les-HERMANS, NEDON & NEDONCHELLE.
    $\frac{A \& B}{20}$ B. F. A. .... NEDONCHELLE
    4th Cavalry .... AMETTES & BELLERY.

NOTE:— The ROUTE NATIONALE de PARIS à DUNKERQUE from LILLERS to the road junction one mile S.E. of FERFAY is outside the Meerut Division billeting area.

2. In consequence of above redistribution, the following movements of troops within the Divisional billeting area, will take place on 25th January 1915:-

(a)

2.

(a) Bareilly Brigade
4th Brigade R.F.A.
130 }
From their present billets to the new Bde billeting area, via:- AMETTES — BELLERY — HURIONVILLE & LILLERS. Rear of column to be clear of BELLERY village by 11.0 A.M. Orders for movement and billeting will be issued by G.O.C. Bareilly Brigade.

13th Bde RFA — Will be on road quarter East of FAUQUEMBERGUES ready by EQUED...10 a.m.

(b) Meerut Divnl Ammn Column
4th Cavalry }
In order given, to their new billeting areas, via HAM — BOURECQ — LESPESSES — LIERES — AMES & BELLERY. The head of the Divnl Ammn Column to leave HAM at 10.30 A.M.

(c) 107th Pioneers
A & B / 26 B.F.A. }
Remain in their present billeting area.

(d) C & D / 26 B.F.A.
(e) 4th Bde RFA }
Will be allocated in the new Bareilly Bde billeting area under the orders of the G.O.C. Bareilly Bde.

3. Refilling will be carried out at BOURECQ at 9.0 A.M. as usual.

The supply wagons of the Divnl Ammn Column and 4th Cavalry will remain at refilling point until their units have passed them, when they will follow their respective units to their new billets.

The supply wagons of the Bareilly Brigade and attached troops will remain at refilling point until the Divnl Ammn Column & 4th Cavalry have passed through, when they will move to their new areas. The G.O.C. Bareilly Brigade will arrange for representatives of units to meet and direct them to the new billets.

4. The G.O.C. Dehra Dun Bde will arrange for orders to be issued for the move of the 9th Brigade R.F.A. into the new Brigade billeting area, to take place before the return of the Garhwal Bde from VIELLE CHAPELLE.

5. Brigade Commdts. will report to Meerut Divn H.Q. as early as possible, the billets allotted to the several units in their respective areas.

G. Noble
Lt. Colonel
General Staff, Meerut Divn.

To,
Bareilly Bde
Garhwal Bde
Dehra Dun Bde
C.R.A.
C.R.E.
4th Cavalry
107th Pioneers

Meerut Signal Coy
Admin. Staff (with 6 spare copies) (for Train, &c. &c.)

No. G/220/2

APPENDIX 74

Headquarters Meerut Division,
23rd January 1914.

Memorandum.

Reference G 220/1 of 22/1/15:—

Para 1.(ii) for "13th Brigade R.F.A." read "4th Brigade R.F.A."

Para 1.(iii) for "4th Brigade R.F.A." read "13th Brigade R.F.A."

Para 2.(a) In margin delete "4th Bde R.F.A."
Insert after "11.0 A.M.":—

"13th Bde R.F.A." — Will clear the road junction on East of FAUQUENHEM village by 10.0 a.m. marching by ECQUEDECQUES." – LILLERS & HANQUEVILLE

Add as para 2.(c):—

"4th Bde R.F.A." — Will follow the march of the Bareilly Brigade (see para 2.(a) above). When the 4th Bde R.F.A. has cleared BELLERY village it will halt on the BELLERY – HURIONVILLE Road until the Divl. Ammn Column and 4th Cavalry (para 2 (b)) have passed through LIERES when it will move into the billets vacated by the 13th Brigade R.F.A.

* Para 1 (iii) For "GUARBECQUE (exclusive)" read "GUARBECQUE inclusive"

C. Rose.
Lt. Col.
General Staff
Meerut Division

To
Bareilly Bde
Garhwal Bde
Dehra Dun Bde
C.R.A.
C.R.E.
4th Cavalry
107th Pioneers
Meerut Signal Coy
Admin. Staff (with six spare copies for Train &c)

APPENDIX 75

No.169-R.A.(L). Headquarters Divisional Artillery,
                 MEERUT Division.

                 24th January 1915.

MEMORANDUM.

The billeting areas of Brigades and Divisional Troops having been re-allotted by MEERUT Division Memoranda Nos.G/22C/A dated the 22nd January 1915 and G/220/S dated 23rd January 1915, the following moves will take place on 25th January 1915:-

1. 13th Brigade R.F.A. from present billets to the BAREILLY Brigade billeting area about HAM. The Brigade will clear the road junction on East of FAUQUEMBERG village by 10.a.m., marching by MOQUEROUQUES and the Northern road junction of LILLERS and MANQUEVILLE.
   Orders for movement and billeting will, it is understood, be issued by G.O.C. BAREILLY Brigade.

2. MEERUT Divisional Ammunition Column to new area at FONTAINE-LES-HERMANS-NEDON and NEDONCHELLE via HAM, BOURECQ-LESPESSES-LILLERS-AMES and BELLERY. The head of the column to leave HAM at 10.30.a.m.

3. 4th Brigade R.F.A. will follow the march of the BAREILLY Brigade (which is moving via AMETTES-BELLERY-HORIONVILLE and LILLERS; rear of this column has received orders to be clear of BELLERY village by 11.a.m.)
   When the 4th Brigade R.F.A. has cleared BELLERY village it will halt on the BELLERY-HORIONVILLE road, until the Divisional Ammunition Column have passed through LILLERS, when it will move into the billets vacated by the 13th Brigade R.F.A. *[and 4th Cavalry]*
   The 4th Cavalry will be moving into billets at AMETTES and BELLERY.

4. The G.O.C. DEHRA DUN Brigade will arrange for orders to be issued for the move of the 4th Brigade R.F.A. into the new Brigade billeting area to take place before the return of the GARHWAL Brigade from VIEILLE CHAPELLE.

5. The Divisional Troops areas have been allotted as follows:-
   (a) Divisional Train................BOURECQ.
       56th How: Battery R.F.A.   )
       110th Heavy Battery R.G.A.) LESPESSES.
   (b) MEERUT Divisional Amn Col: FONTAINE-LES-HERMANS,
                                  NEDON and NEDONCHELLE.
       A & B/24th Brit:Field Ambles NEDONCHELLE.
       4th Cavalry...................AMETTES and BELLERY.
   Note:- The Route Nationale de PARIS à DUNKERQUE from LILLERS to the road junction one mile S.E. of FERFAY is outside the MEERUT Division billeting area.

6. Refilling will be carried out at BOURECQ at 9.a.m. as usual.
   The supply wagons of the Divisional Ammunition Column and 4th Cavalry will remain at refilling point until their units have passed them, when they will follow their respective units to their new billets.
   The supply wagons of the BAREILLY Brigade and attached *troops* will remain at refilling point until the Divisional Ammunition Column and 4th Cavalry have passed through when they will move to their new areas. The G.O.C. BAREILLY Brigade will arrange for representatives of units to meet and direct them to the new billets.

7.

FRANCE (BETHUNE)

(Revised System of Squaring).

COMBINED SHEET 36a S.E. 36 S.W.
36b N.E. 36c N.W.

Scale 1:40,000

Contour Interval 20 Metres

APPENDIX 100

C.R.A. Meerut Divr

WAR DIARY
4.2.15 — 14.2.15
FRANCE.
Scale 1:40,000.
BETHUNE.
COMBINED SHEETS.
36a S.E. 36 S.W.
36b N.E. 36c N.W.
R.A. Meerut Divn

7. MEERUT Division Routine Order No. 64 dated the 30th
January 1915, regarding billeting is republished:-

For paragraph 4 of Routine Order No.157 of 1914,
substitute the following:-

"Before any unit leaves it billeting area the
Officer Commanding should see the MAIRES of all
villages in which any portion of his unit is
billeted and ascertain that all complaints have
been enquired into and disposed of".

Major R.A.,

Brigade Major, Royal Artillery.
MEERUT DIVISION.

To.
The O.C. 4th Brigade R.F.A.
The O.C. 9th Brigade R.F.A.
The O.C. 13th Brigade R.F.A.
The O.C. 58th How: Battery R.F.A.
The O.C. 110th Heavy Battery R.G.A.
O.C.
The/Meerut Divisional Ammunition Column.

Copy to WAR DIARY.

"A" Form.

MESSAGES AND SIGNALS.

No. of Message

APPENDIX 76

Prefix	Code	m.	Words	Charge		This message is on a/c of:	Recd. at	m.
Office of Origin and Service Instructions.			Sent				Date	
			At	m.		Service.	From	
			To				By	
			By		(Signature of "Franking Officer.")			

TO — Genl Staff Mounted Divn

Sender's Number	Day of Month	In reply to Number	AAA
RA 3.24	25.1.15		

Reference G/220/1 dated 23/1/15 para 2 (f) is it essential that Mounted Divnl Amn Column should march through LESPESSES please AAA It is suggested that the route given (there in) but with the omission of the word LESPESSES would be a very much easier route for ammunition wagons and mule carts unless required for other purposes

(Priority)

From	C R A Mounted Divn
Place	HAM
Time	8.30 a.m.

The above may be forwarded as now corrected. (Z)

for CRA

"A" Form.   Army Form C. 2121.

MESSAGES AND SIGNALS.

No. of Message 2

Prefix	Code	m.	Words	Charge	APPENDIX 11	Rec'd. at 9·15 m.
Office of Origin and Service Instructions.			16		This message is on a/c of ?	Date F/G 25/1/15
PRIORITY	At	m.	Sent		Service.	From 1/1/15
	To					By E.F. Schmidt
	By			(Signature of "Franking Officer.")		

TO   CRA

Sender's Number	Day of Month	In reply to Number	AAA
G 220/3	25th	RA 24	

approved aaa omit word LESPESSES from route

From   MEERUT DIVN
Place
Time   9·0 AM

"A" Form.
MESSAGES AND SIGNALS.

APPENDIX 78

TO: O.C. Dev? A.C.

Sender's Number: KAS 25
Day of Month: 25.1.15
AAA

Secret Div? Comd approval of the word "LESPESSES" being omitted from your route AAA This will now read HAM - BOURECQ - LIERES - AMES - & BELLERY. AAA This with reference my 17 KA(L) d 24/1 para 2

From: Bde Major R.A.
Place: HAM
Time: 9.25 a.m.

Form. Army Form C. 2121
AND SIGNALS No. of Message

	Charge	This message is on a/c of:	Recd. at 12.15 P m
	Sent		Date 25/1/15
	At m.	79 Service.	From F/G
	To	(Signature of "Franking Officer.")	By Sinnott
	By		

TO — C R A MEERUT DIVN

| Sender's Number | Day of Month | In reply to Number | AAA |
| G 231/1 | 25th | | |

110 heavy battery to remain in constant state of readiness for next few days AAA acknowledge

From MEERUT DIVN
Place
Time 12·0 NOON

Sinnott

To O.C. 110th (H) Bty R.G.A.

O.C. Div'l A.C.

For information & necessary action
Please acknowledge receipt above.

25/1/15.

P.G. Robinson
Capt RFA
for Brig. Maj. RA

Noted
1.30 p.m.

W. Loring Macookie
Comdg 110 H.Y Bty RGA

C.R.A
For information & return please

P.G. Robinson
Capt RFA
for Brig. Maj. RA

25/1/15

Matthew Jennings
Major RA
Comdg Div Am Col

2.15 pm
25/1/15 Noted

25.1.15

"A" Form.
Army Form C. 2...

MESSAGES AND SIGNALS.

Prefix	Code	m.	Words	Charge	APPENDIX	Recd. at 3.20 P m.
Office of Origin and Service Instructions.			Sent		This message is on a/c of	Date
Priority			At	m.	Service	25/4/15 From
			To			F.C.
			By		(Signature of "Franking Officer.")	By Sinnott

TO — 110th H BTY

Sender's Number	Day of Month	In reply to Number	AAA
1122	25		

Indian Corps No G216 begins send 110th H BTY to 2nd DIVN as soon as possible battery commander to report to 2nd DIVN at Cocon ends for action acknowledged

From MEERUT DIVN
Place
Time

The above may be forwarded as now corrected. (Z)

Censor. Signature of Addressor or person authorised to telegraph in his name

*This line should be erased if not required.

"A" Form.   Army Form C. 2121.

MESSAGES AND SIGNALS.   No. of Message 9

Prefix SB Code R m.	Words 53	Charge APPENDIX 81	Recd. at 3.55 p.m.
Office of Origin and Service Instructions. Y 16 Priority	Sent At m. To By	This message is on a/c of: Service. (Signature of "Franking Officer.")	Date 28/1/15 From Y16 By S. Brown

TO   C R A

| Sender's Number 1123 | Day of Month 25th | In reply to Number | AAA |

Indian Corps no G216 begins send 110th Heavy Battery to Second Division as soon as possible Bty Commander to report to Second division at LOCON ends AAA It should march by LILLERS and BETHUNE and commander should ascertain from Second division where battery will refil supplies tomorrow

Sent 3.55 p.m.

From   MEERUT DIVISION
Place
Time

The above may be forwarded as now corrected.   (Z)

"A" Form. Army Form C.

MESSAGES AND SIGNALS.

No. of Message 5

Prefix SB	Code BP m.	Words 85	Charge	APPENDIX	Recd. at 1·13 P m.
Office of Origin and Service Instructions.		Sent		This message is on a/c of	Date F1G 26/1/15
1G Priority		At m. To By		82 Service. (Signature of "Franking Officer.")	From 1G By Br Staff A

TO { CR A

Sender's Number	Day of Month	In reply to Number	AAA
G.246/1	26th		

Order 56th Howitzer Battery and Ammn Column echelon which supply it to march soon as possible to CALONNE en route to be attached to 4th Corps AAA Commanding Officer to report to HQ 8th Division LA GORGUE today AAA Supply wagons will refil tomorrow at BOURECQ and march to CALONNE where guide should be left to direct wagons to village billets AAA Report hour at which Battery & Brigade and Divnl Amtn Column echelons will march soon as possible

From Meerut Divn
Place
Time 1·10 PM

The above may be forwarded as now corrected. (Z)

Censor. Signature of Addressor or person authorised to telegraph in his name

*This line should be erased if not required.

"A" Form. Army Form C. 2121.
MESSAGES AND SIGNALS.

Prefix SB Code
Words 61
APPENDIX 83

TO: BAREILLY BDE — 104TH PIONEERS
C R A MEERUT

Sender's Number: G244/1
Day of Month: 26
AAA

Orders received from indian corps for devesion to be prepared to move at shortest notice owing this in view of probable presence of fresh german troops in front of british positions acknowledge addressed C R A C R E bareilly bde 4th cavalry and 104th pioneers

From: MEERUT DIVN G
Time: 5.30 PM

"A" Form. Army Form C. 2121.

MESSAGES AND SIGNALS.

No. of Message _____

Prefix **SB** Code _____ m.   Words **33**   Charge _____

Office of Origin and Service Instructions

Sent At _____ m.
To
By

This message is on a/c of:
~~APPENDIX 82~~
Service.
(Signature of "Franking Officer.")

Date _____
From _____
By _____

TO { C R A

Sender's Number **G247/5**   Day of Month **24th**   In reply to Number **G247/1**   **AAA**

Continuation my of 26th AAA maintain your unit in a condition of being able to turn out at two hours notice

Recd 9-10am

From / Place: **MEERUT DIVISION**
Time: **9.48 AM**

The above may be forwarded as now corrected. (Z)

Censor.   Signature of Addresser or person authorised to telegraph in his name

*This line should be erased if not required.

"A" Form. Army Form C. 2121.
MESSAGES AND SIGNALS.
No. of Message 4

APPENDIX 83

Recd. at 1.50 m.
Date 27/1/15
From S/R
By Gen J Stuart

TO: BAREILLY BRIGADE
107 PIONEERS
CRA

Sender's Number: G247/6
Day of Month: 27th
AAA

Following from Indian Corps begins my G239 today under orders from first army only Lahore Divn will be kept in state of readiness aaa of Lahore Divn one brigade will be ready to march at four hours notice remainder will carry on training as usual but arrangements must be made for minimising of delay in turning out remainder orders of division aaa orders being issued regarding grant of leave addressed Lahore and Meerut division ends this cancels oc G247/5 of today

From: MEERUT DIVN
Place:
Time: 1.15 PM